PRAISE FOR

Hot Cripple

"Hogan Gorman has written a smart, tough, and very funny book about serious injury, immense pain, and her war against the American medical system. Oh, and did I mention that it's very *funny*?"

—Salman Rushdie

"Equal parts hilarity and humiliation, funny and frustrating, bone breaks and head shakes, *Hot Cripple* will force you to look more closely at our health care, legal, and social welfare systems, as well as your own life and the lives of those we ignore every day."

—Wade Rouse, author of *It's All Relative*
and *I'm Not the Biggest Bitch in This Relationship*

"Hogan Gorman's story will make you furious, it will make you incredulous, and it will also make you laugh your ass off."

—Rachel Dratch, comedian and
author of *Girl Walks into a Bar . . .*

HOT
Cripple

**An Incurable Smart-ass
Takes on the Health Care System
and Lives to Tell the Tale**

HOGAN GORMAN

A Perigee Book

A PERIGEE BOOK
Published by the Penguin Group
Penguin Group (USA) Inc.
375 Hudson Street, New York, New York 10014, USA

Penguin Group (Canada), 90 Eglinton Avenue East, Suite 700, Toronto, Ontario M4P 2Y3, Canada (a division of Pearson Penguin Canada Inc.) • Penguin Books Ltd., 80 Strand, London WC2R 0RL, England • Penguin Group Ireland, 25 St. Stephen's Green, Dublin 2, Ireland (a division of Penguin Books Ltd.) • Penguin Group (Australia), 250 Camberwell Road, Camberwell, Victoria 3124, Australia (a division of Pearson Australia Group Pty. Ltd.) • Penguin Books India Pvt. Ltd., 11 Community Centre, Panchsheel Park, New Delhi—110 017, India • Penguin Group (NZ), 67 Apollo Drive, Rosedale, Auckland 0632, New Zealand (a division of Pearson New Zealand Ltd.) • Penguin Books (South Africa) (Pty.) Ltd., 24 Sturdee Avenue, Rosebank, Johannesburg 2196, South Africa

Penguin Books Ltd., Registered Offices: 80 Strand, London WC2R 0RL, England

While the author has made every effort to provide accurate telephone numbers and Internet addresses at the time of publication, neither the publisher nor the author assumes any responsibility for errors or for changes that occur after publication. Further, the publisher does not have any control over and does not assume any responsibility for author or third-party websites or their content.

First edition: March 2012

Library of Congress Cataloging-in-Publication Data

Gorman, Hogan.
Hot cripple : an incurable smart-ass takes on the health care system and lives to tell the tale / Hogan Gorman.
        p.   cm.
ISBN 978-0-399-53728-8 (pbk.)
1. Gorman, Hogan—Health.   2. Medical care—United States.   3. Health insurance—
United States.   4. Models (Person)—United States—Biography.   I. Title.
RA412.5.U6G67   2012   2011040438
        368.38'2—dc23

PRINTED IN THE UNITED STATES OF AMERICA

10   9   8   7   6   5   4   3   2   1

This book describes the real experiences of real people. The author has disguised the identities of some and, in some instances, created composite characters, but none of these changes has affected the truthfulness and accuracy of her story. Penguin is committed to publishing works of quality and integrity. In that spirit, we are proud to offer this book to our readers; however, the story, the experiences, and the words are the author's alone.

AUTHOR'S NOTE: Names have been changed to protect the guilty, the innocent, and my own ass. In certain cases, physical appearances have been changed . . . usually for the better (I'm a giver like that).

For my mom

CONTENTS

HOT CRIPPLE

PROLOGUE

Don't hate me because I'm beautiful. Just hate me because I'm better looking than you are. Isn't that what we secretly imagine the pretty woman is thinking as she elegantly walks by us on the street? Your thought process probably goes something like this (unless of course you're a man, and then you only have one thought: *hot*):

She's tall . . . I hate her.

She's blonde . . . she's probably stupid, and I hate her.

She's thin in an "I've worked out every day of my life" sort of way . . . I definitely hate her.

Love her outfit . . . God I wish I had that dress . . . HATE HER.

* * *

Well, I'm "her." I'm a five-foot-ten, blue-eyed blonde, and weigh 120 dripping wet. I used to be a model, but I got bored with that and decided I needed a real, dependable job, so I became an actress. I have a closet full of clothes to end all closets; well, actually, my clothes are overflowing and strategically hung all over my bed-room, which resembles a boudoir or maybe a high-end garage sale. I'm not going to lie; life is pretty good. I'm happy and healthy. God, I never thought I'd say those words again.

I guess I should start by introducing myself, and then we'll have to backtrack a little . . . Trust me, you won't be hating me for much longer.

Hi, I'm Hogan. Yes, I know, a rather unusual name for a woman, but my brother's name is Spike, and quite frankly, I think I got the better end of the deal. I am in no way related to Hulk, Paul, or Ben Hogan, nor do I have a goat. I do, however, have a few heroes.

Let's journey back to 2004, which according to Wikipedia was a leap year, Bush was up for reelection, the United Nations designated it "the year of rice," and the World Health Organization declared the 2004 World Health Day Topic "Road Safety" (you're going to find that last fact ironic in a minute, so remember it).

Like most actors in New York, I was a slasher (actress-slash-waitress). But not a waitress like at your local diner or restaurant. I'm an ex-model—what the hell do I know about food? I decided drunks were more my speed, so I became a cocktail waitress. My workdays started when most people were winding down their days, and ended when some people were starting theirs. I worked in nightclubs—you know, the ones with the imposing doormen behind the velvet ropes, with the guest lists that you would give your first-born child to be on. Sure, it sounds glamorous, but trust me, it wasn't—unless you like being treated like an indentured servant. I have been whistled at, had fingers snapped at me, and literally been barked at, all just to get my attention. I've had drinks spilled on me, had drinks thrown at me, and been burned by cigarettes, all courtesy of the inebriated. I have had my toe broken and my toenail torn off, due to a drunken slut falling off a table while dancing in stiletto heels. I have had a prince from the Middle East offer my manager a brand-new BMW if he would give me to him to be his seventh wife. Just like being in a burka while strapped to the back of a camel didn't sound glamorous to me, neither was being a cocktail waitress. Besides these albatrosses around my neck, there were also things that I was forced to live without. Health insurance was a big one. Night clubs don't offer health care, and between rent and food, as well as an unstable income based mostly on tips, I couldn't afford it on my own. I convinced myself that I would be fine without insurance; I was healthy, I worked out, and besides a seasonal cold I never got sick. There was also absolutely no job security; they could fire you at any given moment without reason. But it did offer me one thing that no other job could: my days free to pursue my acting, and flexibility if I needed to take off a couple of weeks to shoot an independent film or do a play (for no money—struggling actors have to take the jobs as they come and hope they lead to something better). I wasn't one of those models-turned-actresses who thought they could act just because they were born physically attractive; I had studied, I was studying, and I planned to continue studying, because acting is a craft, not one long photo shoot. I was merely supporting myself nocturnally until my acting could support me.

I became part of what I like to call the Cocktail Mafia, a group of six girls that traveled in a pack from hot spot to hot spot. You could rest assured that if a hip new club was opening, we would be your waitresses. The other Mafia members were a wealth of entertainment, but that doesn't mean I considered them friends. I had nicknames for them all, which I kept to myself of course:

The Heiress was convinced that she was born into the wrong family. She was from Brazil and an admitted gold digger, and if you were a member of the Fortune 500, she already knew your address and your Social Security number.

Sylvia Plath was a poet and German. Need I say more? *Happy* was not a word in this girl's vocabulary. If she made five hundred dollars in a night, she would end up going home and crying and writing a poem about the injustice of the American economy.

Gidget was young and fun and fresh out of college, and she just loved being a cocktail waitress. "Perky" is the perfect description; she made coffee look sedate. Nobody is naturally that up and bubbly. I was hoping whatever she was on, she could give me some and I could slip it into Sylvia's drink. Although the thought of two Gidgets was really frightening.

The Southern Belle was someone you could picture sipping mint juleps on the veranda. She had the face of an angel, and she was genuinely sweet. She also had an obsession with hip-hop music and called everybody "Girl," which was funny because she was the most Wonder bread person on the planet. Those Southern women do the damsel-in-distress thing so well, and she had perfected it to a science.

The Vixen would put Pamela Anderson to shame. She had curves in all the right places. Her two most prominent curves were bought and paid for by her ex-boyfriend . . . and when the going got tough, the Vixen would apply lip gloss. A fight could break out in the club, with bottles flying and tables flipping over, and all her customers yelling at her for their checks, and she would just stop and get a faraway look in her eyes, and out would come the lip gloss. I was amazed at the way she could totally remove herself from a stressful situation with no other aid. It was kind of like Buddhism for Barbies.

Every Mafia has a Don, and we were no different. This little spitfire from south of the border would work nine out of seven days to support her entire family back in the motherland. She was a natural-born leader, or dictator, as the case may be. Any time we had a disagreement, I was sure I was going to come home and find a horse head in my bed. This chiquita didn't play around.

At first I kept my distance from these girls, but over time I found myself liking them—in a Stockholm syndrome sort of a way—that is, until the night I almost killed a customer. It was Luau Night at the club, and some pervert tried to untie my bikini top. I lunged around and grabbed the perpetrator by the Adam's apple, digging my fingernails into his throat and walking him slowly backward toward the front door while repeating my mantra: "I love my life, I love my job, I love my life, I love my job." At this point, my favorite bouncer, Big John, came up.

"Sunshine, do we have a problem?" he asked as he gently removed my hand from the perpetrator's throat.

"This fucker untied my bikini while I was waiting on a table," I replied as I tried to regain my grip around the pervert's neck.

"Okay, I'll take it from here . . . Now, sunshine, I want you to go over there and take ten deep breaths."

I knew something was wrong if a bouncer was giving me anger-management tips. I was over cocktail waitressing with a capital OVER. This suffering thing really wasn't my bag. I thought this job would last a few months until I got my big break and be a cute story to tell Barbara or Oprah, but a few months had become a few years. I was losing the plot, and I knew it. I was having an existential crisis.

I decided to bounce this crisis off my friend Aura. She's very peace, love, and patchouli. I met her at her favorite macroneurotic restaurant, for a bowl of air and a cup of steam with the dressing on the side. I hadn't even taken the first bite of my rather unappetizing seaweed (and God knows what else) salad when Aura informed me that my energy seemed a little off and demanded in her Hacky Sack sort of a way to know what was going on.

"I'm sick of waitressing, but the money is good and I have the rest of the week to go on auditions. That is, if there *were* any auditions. I haven't had an acting job in six months. Maybe I should go to L.A. . . . but the amount of Botox and number of Ugg boots in L.A. makes the Cocktail Mafia look like Gloria Steinem. I hate my life right now."

To which Aura countered, "No, remember, you love your life and you love your job."

I didn't want to tell Aura that I had used her mantra the other night and almost strangled a customer, and that it clearly wasn't working out for me. How I wished I could be Zen like her, in a permanent, naturally stoned state of euphoria, but I wasn't. I was waiting on pseudo-heterosexual drunken slobs and the tarts who date them when I should have been acting. I hated my life, and I hated my job.

Aura continued her rainbow-and-unicorn moment. "What you need to do is ask the universe for a change. I'm telling you, if you put it out there, the universe will give you a change. I know you always feel that you have to do everything on your own, but you don't. Let the universe help you."

The definition of *desperate*, according to *Webster's*, is: "Moved by despair, involving or employing extreme measures in an attempt to escape defeat or frustration." And I was there. "I love my life, I love my job" was hippie-dippy at best, but now my granola friend wanted me to talk to the universe?

But I'll try anything once—usually some weird food or sexual position—so I figured what the hell. For the next week in the privacy of my tiny shoe-box apartment, I would say at least a few times a day, "Universe, I need a change," or "Universe, bring on a change." I felt silly but . . . (see above definition).

Unfortunately, the universe was actually listening for once . . .

CHAPTER ONE

Be Careful What You Wish For

It's March 4, 2004, and I am off to my own personal hell for the evening, otherwise known as my waitressing job. Every night I work I have the same ritual: I take a cab from my house to the Starbucks at Astor Place, which is a block away from the nightclub, to get my grande soy, no water, no foam, Tazo chai. That's Starbucks-speak for tea. Tonight is no different. I stand in line behind a couple of NYU students and patiently wait my turn.

"You having the usual?" Robbie, my favorite barista, asks. I love that he wears eyeliner, and he smudges it to perfection.

"Yep."

"Grande soy, no water, no foam, Tazo chai," he calls out. "You working tonight?"

"Ugh. Yeah. I can't wait till I don't have to waitress anymore."

"I feel ya, girl. One of these days I'm gonna come in and have a drink," he says with a smile, ringing me up for a much less expensive coffee.

"You better. Then I can buy you a drink for once. See ya, Robbie," I say as I grab my chai and walk out the door. It's a crisp March evening, the kind that says the worst of the winter is behind us and spring will be approaching soon. I have my favorite Earl corduroy jacket on, which is a pleasant change after months of wearing winter coats. The cocktail dress and heels I wear as my work uniform are packed neatly in my bag, and I am enjoying the last few minutes of comfort in my Juicy jeans and T-shirt as I walk down the block to work. I don't really feel like working tonight . . . Who am I kidding? I never feel like waitressing. Oh crap, I forgot to do Aura's little mantra today. I've been doing it at least a few times a day for the past week. I quickly look around to see if anyone is within earshot, and luckily the coast is clear. "Universe, I am ready for a change," I mutter. For the first time I am really starting to believe a change is coming. I step off the curb and begin to cross Lafayette Street. The nightclub is straight in front of me, when . . .

BOOM!

I'M IN THE AIR . . .

EVERYTHING IS MOVING IN SLOW MOTION . . .

THE SOUND OF BREAKING GLASS . . .

MY HEAD . . . OH MY HEAD . . .

SCREECHING BRAKES . . .

I'M IN THE AIR AGAIN . . .

OWW!

PAVEMENT.

MY BACK . . . MY HEAD . . .

I want to yell for help, but nothing comes out. I'm in the far lane of traffic on my back. Everything is blurry. I hear people:

"Are you okay?"

"I saw everything. I'm calling nine-one-one."

"Oh my God, it's Hogan. Call her brother! But first call some-one to cover her shift."

"We've got to get you out of the street."

Hands lift me. I'm on the sidewalk. The car is ten feet away from me, and there is no glass in the back windshield, except for one small shard in the lower left-hand corner with my grande soy, no water, no foam, Tazo chai impaled on it.

"Oh my God," I say. "My head took out an entire windshield."

I can't stop crying.

The people who hit me get out of a four-door Mercedes, two couples in their mid- to late-forties. The woman from the passen-ger side is running toward me. Now, one would assume that if you just hit someone with your car while you were driving in reverse at an uncontrollable speed down a one-way street, and that she is clearly injured, considering her head just took out your back wind-shield, you would be concerned for her life, right? Wrong. The passenger from hell starts yelling at me. "Stand up! You're not hurt! I'm a doctor—I know you're not hurt!"

By now there are at least ten people on the street that have come out of my place of employment and the restaurant next door. Two people get the crazy woman away from me, one person is writing down the license plate number, and another is trying to convince my only eyewitness to give him his contact information. I, on the other hand, am lying on the sidewalk and trying not to vomit.

AMBULANCE . . .

SIRENS . . .

POLICE LIGHTS . . .

You know those moments when something really horrible is happening in a dream? You're falling off a building, getting chased by a serial killer, whatever? I am having one of those moments. "Wake up . . . this isn't real . . . it's just a bad dream . . . this could never happen to you . . . wake up," I keep telling myself in an attempt to pull out of this nightmare.

"I can't believe you're alive. When I saw the car I was sure you were a DOA. Your shirt's real funny . . . 'Dump Him,' that's real funny," says the EMT, as he straps me to a board and neck collar and puts me in the ambulance, but not before first hitting my head on the ambulance door.

Did your mom always warn you to wear clean underwear in case you were in an accident? I begin racking my brain to figure out if I am wearing the presentable part of my lingerie drawer. I am jarred out of my Victoria's Secret conundrum by my brother, who enters the back of the ambulance with all the grace of a bull in a china shop. My brother always tries to hide the fact that he is losing his shit, but when he does he paces. It's rather impossible to pace in the back of an ambulance, but he is somehow managing to accomplish this feat, and now I know that not only is this not a dream but it's bad. "Thank God . . . Hoge . . . you're alive. I got here as fast as I could, and I saw the car and the glass all over and I thought you were dead. Those people that hit you were laughing like it was a joke, and one of them told the police that you jumped on their car and elbowed their windshield out. I didn't see you, and I thought they'd killed you. I was getting ready to beat the crap out of them when the cop told me you were in the ambulance. Fuck! Dude, you're going to be okay, you're going to be okay."

At this point I start to hyperventilate . . . I'm not sure if it is because two people have just told me in the past five minutes that there is no way I should be alive right now, or the fact that it is really sinking in that I, Little Miss Never Broke a Bone in Her Life, just got mowed down by a car. The short, stocky EMT notices that I am gasping for air like someone in the last stages of emphysema and informs me in his thick New Jersey accent that I am in shock. He tries to help me regulate my breathing with his version of a guided meditation. "Slow, slow, breathe, breathe." It is like Joe Pesci leading a Lamaze class.

In the hospital I am still strapped to a board and in a neck collar, so I can only see the ceiling. The ER nurse and the EMT proceed to make small talk, like two old friends catching up at a coffee klatch. They cover a variety of topics: what they had for dinner, Internet dating, and a recent vacation. Finally, after five minutes, the nurse acknowledges the fact that I am lying below them on a gurney in the hospital hallway. "So what have we got here?"

"Pedestrian, struck by a car going approximately forty miles per hour. Her head went through and completely shattered the windshield, and then she was thrown approximately ten feet, landing on the pavement and hitting her cervical, lumbar, and head," says the EMT, as if he were reciting the daily lunch specials in a New Jersey diner.

In the emergency room I am staring at the fluorescent light above my head and listening to my brother pace. I have to say something to calm him down. "Hey, I'm like that girl in the neck brace in that John Hughes film . . . What was that film?"

He stops pacing for a minute to think out loud. "Oh yeah, remember when she tries to drink from the water fountain but she can't move her neck, and keeps hitting herself in the face with the water? What the hell was it called?"

The guy on the gurney next to me answers, "*Sixteen Candles*."

I must be losing my mind, or I'm dead and purgatory is a game show called *Emergency Room Jeopardy*.

I'm waiting, and waiting. My head is pounding. The pain is going down my arms and legs. My feet are numb.

Finally, the doctor, whose beady eyes and big front teeth put me in mind of a gopher, comes. He shines a light in my eyes and has me wiggle my fingers and my toes. "All right, I'm going to have your brother fill out your insurance information and then we'll send you right up to X-ray."

"I'm a waitress . . . I don't have insurance."

"Oh, no insurance?" he says with an exasperated look on his face, removing his eyes from me and staring at his clipboard. "Okay, well, someone will take you up . . . eventually."

"Can I at least have something for the pain?"

"Here you go," he replies, handing me a pill.

"What is it?" I whimper as he walks away.

"Tylenol."

The trivia whiz in the bed next to me fainted during dinner, and all the nurses and doctor are paying attention to him. "Can we get you something to drink, Mr. Smith?" "We're going to give you more pain medication, Mr. Smith." "We're going to rush you right up for a CAT scan, Mr. Smith."

The only person who pays attention to me is Andy the EMT, who keeps coming back to the emergency room to check on me between drop-offs. "Your shirt's real funny . . . 'Dump Him.' So I guess you're single. How can a girl like you be single?"

Note to self: Along with wearing presentable undergarments,

add to the list: never wear a shirt that advertises your availability across your tits.

After Andy's second visit, I ask my pacing brother if he thinks the EMT is hitting on me, which elicits a chuckle. "Hoge, you're a cute girl, but you're not looking too cute right now. You have streaks of mascara down your face, you're strapped to a board in a neck brace, and your hair is doing this Don King thing."

I slowly reach my hand up to the matted mess that I once called hair. "Oh my God, is this blood?"

With trepidation, my brother moves closer to examine, and then bends down and smells my head. "No, sweetie, that's your chai tea. I can't believe they haven't even bothered to get the glass out of your hair."

He returns to his pacing, and then gets a call and walks out of the emergency room. I'm not sure if he is doing it to obey the signs that say "No cell phones." He's never been one to follow rules, so I'm guessing he doesn't want me to hear the conversation. It's probably my mom. She is completely going to freak out. When my mom reads the paper she starts with the obituaries, and if she hears someone has cancer, she has them mentally buried and is already thinking of what she is going to wear to the funeral. People of Irish descent are big on potatoes, not optimism.

God, I wish she were here. I don't care how old you are; sometimes you just need your mom.

A weepy moment ensues . . . which I am sure is exacerbating my mascara problem.

Trivia Whiz is back from X-ray and CAT scan. I decide to eavesdrop on the doctor's prognosis (not that I have any choice, considering there is only a sheet separating us). "Okay, Mr. Smith, we got the results back from your CAT scan and everything looks fine, but we're going to keep you overnight for observation. We have all your insurance information, and Bob is going to take you up to your room right now."

I go back to focusing on my own pain, which is getting worse. My entire body is throbbing, and I'm getting stabbing pains in my head. Am I dying? Not that anyone would notice, mind you.

Most people are completely terrified of hospitals, and while I'll admit that they smell sterile and their paint selections are rather limited to blinding white and that putrid Band-Aid color, I've spent some quality time at hospitals in my youth. Well, there is the obvious occasion—my birth—which I have no recollection of, but I have seen pictures and would like to thank my mother's OB-GYN, because although I was born a cone head, his skillful hands shaped my malleable skull like Michelangelo formed the *David*, and thanks to him I now have a head that in no way resembles an alien's.

At two, I took my second trip to the hospital. My mother had given me some loose change as a reward for graduating from diapers to big-girl panties. She was no dummy . . . She knew that if she bought me—a girly-girl through and through—the prettiest, laciest underwear, there was no way I was going to mess them. No coaching, no accidents, just me and my cute girl undies. I put my reward on my bedside table to spend at the candy store the next day. I awoke my mother in a panic that night, gasping for air. I had had a rather lucid dream in which I was a bubble gum machine and swallowed a penny in my sleep. Yes, easily potty trained but clearly not the sharpest tool in the shed. The penny was lodged in my esophagus, which required them shoving the Jaws of Life down my throat and extracting it. On a high note, the doctor gave my mother my prescription: Popsicles and pudding for a week, and no more change . . . I was upgraded to dollar bills.

In my third year of life, I had my third visit to the emergency room. We were over at my mother's friend's house so I could have a play date with her son, who had a hobbyhorse in the back garden with my name all over it. I rode that thing like Seabiscuit until the demon son pushed me off, demanding his toy back. My chin was split open, getting blood all over my favorite eyelet dress. And as I tore up the stairs to the house bellowing for my mother, with Satan's spawn following, fearful that he was going to get in trouble, I turned around and *gently* pushed him down the flight of stairs . . . so it was a group emergency room play date. The little shit had a broken nose, and I was stitched up without the benefit of a plastic surgeon. My mother still feels guilty over that one, but I kinda like my little Harrison Ford chin scar.

My fourth, fifth, sixth, and seventh trips to the hospital were due to my brother and his childhood affliction of croup, which caused his vocal cords to swell and make him bark like a seal. When vaporizers or throwing him in a steamy bathroom failed to open up his breathing, we would speed off to the hospital with my brother's head hanging out the car window. I wasn't allowed in the emergency room, so my mother would leave me in the waiting room to be watched by the inmates of San Quentin Prison, who were usually there after getting in a knife fight. I guess she figured they were adequate babysitters considering they were handcuffed and shackled. And after being forced to play Barbies with me, I bet they were pretty excited to head back to prison. My mother and newly breathing brother would eventually emerge from the emergency room, and I would say good-bye to my captive play-

mates, promising that the next time they could be Barbie and not
Skipper.

When I was a tweenie, my mother started working at a hospital as an administrative assistant (which sounded like a very fancy
title to me). On a few chosen days in the summer I was allowed to
accompany my mother to work, which was pure heaven. This job
was much better than her last one: working for so-called tree experts, who would cut down people's sick trees (or something to
that effect; I was never exactly sure what they did). Here they
helped sick *people*, and that was far cooler in my *Teen Beat* mind.
I would help my mom file papers, draw rainbows and fluffy cloud
pictures for her coworkers, roam the halls of the hospital pretending I was visiting a relative, say hello to the doctors, go see the
babies in the maternity ward, make several trips to the gift shop
looking to increase my sugar level to get through the long, exciting workday, and drop in on my favorite medical librarian (who
my mom informed me was far smarter than all the doctors) . . .
and that was all before lunch, which was the best part of the day.
In the hospital cafeteria surrounded by the doctors and nurses
in their scrubs, I would sit with my mother and her friends, quietly thinking that this was the greatest place in the world, and
surely the safest.

At the age of thirteen I had my one and only experience as an
in-patient. I had joined a ski club. There was another girl in the
club; her name ended in a *y*, as all cute girls' names do. She had
perfectly glossed Bonne Bell lips, her breath always smelled like
peppermint as the result of her addiction to breath spray, she was
ideally petite and cute at five-four, the boys had discovered her,
and, most important, she was a great skier. I, on the other hand,

was five-ten (taller than my principal and all the boys); I had just gotten my braces off, which caused me to constantly run my tongue across my teeth and chap my lips (no amount of Bonne Bell was helping me); and although I was athletic, I had yet to get off the intermediate slopes. But that wasn't stopping me . . . I was going to beat this perfect bitch on skis if it was the last thing I did. So when she said, "Hey, Hogan, do you want to ski Devil's Run today? I mean, if you're up to it?" I took that as a dare, maybe even a double dare.

The accident involved me, an icy mogul, and four flips. My knee went one way while my skis and unreleased bindings went the other, and Little Miss Bonne Bell with a *y* elegantly plowed snow in my face as she skied past me. I rode back on the bus with a cardboard makeshift splint on my leg, a messed-up knee, and a severely bruised ego. By the time I got home, my mother had already arranged for a doctor from the hospital to come over and examine me on my embarrassing canopy bed. She also had some keen words of advice. "Sweetheart, the next time you're jealous of a cheerleader type, why don't you try doing something normal like spreading a rumor about her, rather than throwing yourself down a mountain."

Two days later I was scheduled for arthroscopic surgery. You would have thought the Queen of England had arrived at the hospital. I had flowers waiting in my private room, all my mom's coworkers came up to greet me, and the nurse informed me that I wouldn't have to eat the normal hospital food; they would let me select from the daily specials in the cafeteria. This was way better than summer camp.

The doctor who would be performing my surgery was the leading surgeon for the 49ers football team, which was impressive—until I met his resident, Dr. D, who was the most beautiful man I had ever seen in my thirteen years of life. He was Calvin Klein–model gorgeous, and I needed to make him mine. Sure, there was the slight age difference of about fifteen years, but math really wasn't my thing, except when calculating that I would be in the hospital for a week. Seven days times twenty-four hours in a day equaled 168 hours to make Dr. D fall head-over-stethoscope.

The morning of the surgery my mother arrived bright and early, panicked, as only a mother can be, that her baby girl was going under the knife. I, on the other end of the spectrum, was relaxed because I was going to spend the morning in close proximity to that paragon of male perfection, Dr. D. That is, until the orderly arrived to prep me for surgery. He was a rather large black man with a smile that made you feel like you had just gotten enveloped in sunshine. "Hello, darlin'. My name is Lou, and I'm here to get you ready for surgery. Now, I'm going to give you a sedative."

I liked Lou; he was the kind of person that you just wanted to know because no matter how blue you were, he would make you feel better. I needed a friend like that in my life, I thought, as he gave me the tranquilizer. Until he said the words that struck horror in my thirteen-year-old heart: "Now, little lady, you need to take off your underwear for surgery."

"No way, man! The underwear stays!" I said with the proper thirteen-year-old roll of the eyes. No way did I want Dr. D to see my business. He would think I was a slut like Debbie Morris, who was so easy-access she probably didn't even *own* underwear.

My mother interjected, "Sweetheart, you need to go into the bathroom and take off your underwear."

"NO!"

"Don't you embarrass me in front of this nice man. You go into the bathroom and take your underwear off for Christ's sake."

"FINE," I replied with venom as I whipped off my panties and threw them out the bathroom door, where they unfortunately landed on Lou's head.

"Hogan Gorman!" my mother exclaimed, trying to sound stern to cover up her laughter.

"It's okay, ma'am. I have a daughter about her age," Lou offered, as he wheeled my gurney into the elevator. "And don't you worry, little lady. You'll be feeling no pain in a few minutes."

"Yeah, Lou . . . I don't give a fuck what they do to me."

"Jesus, Hogan! I have to work here," my mother said, dying of embarrassment.

The next three days were a blur, but apparently I was doing my best Linda Blair impersonation until my mother demanded that they cut off my Demerol after I threw my lunch in her face. Once I was lucid and coherent, my mother took great pleasure in recapping the past few days. "I was in the cafeteria today and Sue the recovery room nurse shouted across the room, 'Hey, Ann, how's your little foul-mouth doing? She was very entertaining in surgery.' And I think you scared the hell out of Dr. D."

I was quite positive I had scared the hell out of Dr. D, and I doubted that being commando in surgery had anything to do with it. I would make a mental note at the tender age of thirteen that drugs turned me into a vulgar, dirty whore. I did, however, like the hospital. I felt protected under the watchful eye of health care professionals. They were smart and caring and reliable, and all they wanted was for me to get better.

Whoever was in charge of such things at the hospital knew my mother was a struggling single mom, and they miraculously never charged her for my week stay, the surgery, or the two months of physical therapy. It pays to work at a hospital; they take care of their own. The only person that charged her was the anesthesiologist, who my mother lovingly referred to as "that asshole" for the next year and a half that it took her to pay him off.

~~~~~~

Back in my present-day emergency room and thinking of asshole doctors—Where is the doctor? I just got hit by a car, people. What happened to the bedside manner of yesteryear? I want to be given Popsicles and pudding for a week, I want to get stitched up, I want to play Barbies with prisoners, I want some drugs, I want my mom to still work at a hospital, I want to be surrounded by her coworkers that gave a shit, I WANT SOME MEDICAL ATTENTION FOR CHRIST'S SAKE. This hospital is terrifying the hell out of me. It's like McDonald's: over a billion served, with inadequate care and goods that could kill you. This is McFucking crazy.

Finally, after several hours, they take me to Radiology, where three guys almost drop me while moving me from the gurney to the table. They x-ray and CAT-scan my neck and back only. "Are you a dancer? You have the body of a dancer," one of them asks as they start to wheel me back to the ER.

"CAT-scan . . . head," I mumble.

"Sorry, we only have orders from the doctor to do your back and neck, so we'll take you down to the ER and you can talk to him."

More waiting.

When the doctor finally shows up, I tell him that they didn't CAT-scan my head, and he says, "Oh, do you think we should?"

I am starting to wonder if this guy got his medical license out of a Cracker Jack box. I muster all I have left and shout, "HEAD, WINDSHIELD, CAT SCAN, NOW!"

I wait another hour.

The doctor returns with the CAT scan results and his ever-present clipboard. "Okay, well the CAT scan showed you do have trauma to the head. It's hard to tell the extent of the damage right now, but you definitely have a concussion. You should get that neck and back looked at by a specialist. Now I'm going to put this neck brace on you and you can go home."

"Home? Home? You want me to go home? That other guy only fainted and he's not going home," I say, truly stunned, before the reality hits me with almost as much force as the car. "Oh . . . I get it . . . he has insurance."

The doctor doesn't answer me. He won't even look at me when he puts on the neck brace. His parting remark is, "Now, the pain will get worse over the next few days. All right, good luck."

My brother manages to get me home. I decline his offer to spend the night. I haven't slept in a bed with my brother since I was eight, and from what I remember, he kicked me in his sleep and I woke up with his elbow in my face. With the amount of pain I am in, I don't want to subject myself to any more bodily harm.

I gimp into my apartment and hear the phone ringing. Even the ring sounds panicked, so I know immediately that it is my mom (who, incidentally, always introduces herself on the phone as if I wouldn't recognize her thick Midwestern, slightly nasal voice after a lifetime of hearing it). "Ohhh . . . sweetheart. It's Mom. Your brother called me. Oh, honey, I can't believe this happened.

I tried to get online to book a ticket, but you know me and computers. I was so upset, I almost threw the damn thing out the window. But I called Pam, and she's going to book me a ticket for tomorrow night. I mean, Christ, I'll grow wings and fly if I have to."

"You don't need to come. I'm all right," I eke out before I burst into tears. I don't know if I'm all right, I just don't want her to panic. I don't know anything right now. It's all too surreal, too strange. "I just want to go to sleep."

"No, honey. Didn't they tell you at the hospital that with a concussion you shouldn't go to sleep?" I tell her no. "He didn't? Piece of shit! I want to kill that fucking doctor. Well, sweetheart, why don't you turn on the TV to something that will keep you awake? . . . Fox News, you always yell at the TV when that's on."

"I'm injured enough; I don't want to be lied to."

"Well, I could just stay on the phone and talk to you all night so you don't fall asleep. Are you sure you don't want me to come?"

"You have to work, and you don't have the money. I'll be okay."

"Don't you worry about that . . . as you say, 'Work can kiss my ass.' So, if you decide you want me, you just let me know and I'll be on the next plane."

I need to get off the phone. The more I talk the more I am panicking her and myself, and I can't keep this stiff-upper-lip thing going for another minute. "Mom, I'm gonna go now. I love you."

"I love you, too," she responds, her voice crackling with emotion.

I hang up the phone, and for the first time tonight, it is quiet.

There are no sounds of screeching brakes or shattering glass or sirens, no beeping medical machines, dismissive doctors, or worried family members. There is just me and the sound of my crying as I hug my baby blanket like a two-year-old and quietly hope that this is just a bad dream.

CHAPTER TWO

Oh, How the Mighty Have Fallen . . . Now That's Just Cruel

The emergency room doctor was right about one thing: the pain is worse. My tiny one-bedroom apartment might as well be the size of a football field. Climbing the four stairs to my bedroom is like scaling Mount Everest. Every step is an effort. I can't stand up straight. I can't move my neck. My right knee has swollen to the size of a softball and is a pretty shade of purple and green, not to be confused with the bruise on my lower back and butt that is the size of Texas. The whole back of my head is one big, swollen, throbbing lump. I am popping Vicodin like candy, and it's not even making a dent in the pain department. It's official: I am a mess.

Then there is the sleep factor, or lack thereof. Every time I close my eyes I replay the accident over in my head, as if my brain is stuck on a loop. I experience every aspect: the sounds of screeching brakes and shattering glass; the feeling of my jaw clenching on impact and my body slamming against the metal. I see my head going through the windshield and finally my body smashing into the cold, hard asphalt. The confusion. The fear. The disbelief. I experience it all as if it were happening all over again, and it does at least four times a night, like *Groundhog Day*. It always ends the same, with the woman yelling at me, "Stand up! You're not hurt! I'm a doctor—I know you're not hurt!" I am startled awake by her words, at which point I proceed to burst into tears. The first time this happens I cry while it dawns on me that this is not just a nightmare, this actually happened. THIS IS A LIFEMARE. Then I cry about the woman. How could someone be so insensitive, callous, vicious, and uncaring, as to yell at a person whom your husband just mowed down with a car? What did I ever do to you? I was just walking to work; it's not like I intended to have my head christen your windshield. You'll get a new windshield, but where do I get a new body? At this point I call her a cunt. And with that . . . I wipe my tears and call this pity party a wrap.

The Cocktail Mafia are calling to check on me, all except the Heiress, who is probably busy digging gold out of some poor Wall Streeter's pockets.

The first to call is the Don, which is appropriate, since she is, after all, the self-appointed leader of the Mafia (in an Eva Braun sort of a way). The other girls practically salute when she walks in the room and hang on her every word, although it can be a bit hard to understand her at times, with her thick Latin accent and raspy voice. Talking to her on the phone is almost impossible without her rather large hand movements to help decode. "Ogan ow are jew?"

"I'm hanging in there," I reply in my most stoic voice.

"Well, wen do jew think jew'll be back at work?"

"Um, I don't know . . . I can barely get from my bedroom to the kitchen right now."

"O jew poor thing. Well, I can cober jew're shifts until jew feel better."

And just like that, they all start circling like vultures over my waitressing shifts.

Next up is the Vixen, and let's just say it's a little hard to have a phone conversation with a woman whose breast size is far larger than her IQ. Then the Southern Belle, doing her best Scarlett O'Hara: "O-o-ohhh girrlll. Aah juuussstt caaan't believeee thisss happeneddd. If youuu needdd anyy littleee thinggg, youuu juuussstt letttt meee knooowww."

Really? I could use some medical insurance, a full body cast, and a gun in my mouth to ease the pain . . . but frankly, my dear, I don't think you give a damn.

Sylvia Plath is despondent as usual, and I think she is a little worried that I am going to steal her depressive thunder. Yes, I have been hit by a car, but she is a dark, German poetess, and holds the Debbie Downer title belt. She is, however, the only one who doesn't ask to cover my waitressing shifts, because in her mind every night she works there sucks the marrow from her bones.

And finally is Gidget, perky as ever in her Valley Girl way: "Oh my God, Hoges, I can't believe this happened . . . I was thinking (a dangerous concept) that I could cover your shifts until you're better. (Wow, what a revolutionary idea.) Oh, and the girls and I took up a collection out of our tips, and I'm going to bring it over to you."

I know none of the others will come because they don't get out of bed until six at night. That being said, it is a very nice gesture. We do make those occasionally, although we have to guilt one another into them. When the Don's father unexpectedly offed himself and she had to fly back to the motherland, we tipped her out every night she would have worked, and by the time she got back, we had an envelope with fifteen hundred dollars in it for her. And birthdays were obscene; I was slightly morally opposed to those, as we'd each lay out an entire night's tips for a gift, which I would have preferred to use toward my rent. But I couldn't say anything because I was outnumbered; go against the Mafia, and I'd be working the graveyard shift at TGI Fridays. I guess my Mafia name is the Outsider. I have aspirations, goals, dreams, and they have nightclubs and other nocturnal endeavors. Except for Sylvia; she has her depression and an eye on the oven.

Gidget bounces into my apartment as if she were going to perform a cheerleading routine. "Hoges, you look . . ." She pauses. She can't say "great," or even "good," because I don't look even remotely close to good or great.

"Like shit," I offer, trying to stop her mental dictionary before she spews out an adjective that we both know is a lie.

"NO . . . you look hurt, very hurt . . . Hurt." She goes in for a hug, but not just any hug . . . a powerful perky bear hug. I am quite sure she just cracked a rib, which is the only part of my body that isn't already injured. I don't want to be mean, or scream in pain; she is here to bring me money after all.

"Can you please let go? It's nice to see you, but you're hurting me," I squeak.

"Oh my God . . . Sorry, Hoges." Taking an envelope out of her purse, she hands it to me. "Here. This is for you. We hope it helps. They took you off the schedule . . . you know?"

"Thanks for this, and please thank the other girls for me," I say, taking the envelope. I choose to ignore the schedule comment. I had figured that would happen rather rapidly. It is official: I am no longer a member of the Cocktail Mafia. I have always known this day would come. I have hoped and prayed it would come. But in my head this wasn't the way I pictured it going down. In my fantasy I would go out in a blaze of glory . . . The nightclub would be in full swing, with a tragically hip New York crowd drinking Cristal champagne, and Grey Goose bottles on every table. The Cocktail Mafia would be in the waitress station having their usual inane conversations, and I would be looking bored but extremely beautiful. Magically, a spotlight would shine down on me just as the Coen brothers are walking into the club. They immediately see me and approach. Joel speaks first: "We are shooting a new film, and you are perfect for the female lead."

"Really?" I say in a nonchalant way. "When's the audition?"

Ethan interrupts, "No need to audition. We heard about your work . . . We can tell just by looking at you that you're a talented and gifted actress. Oh, I guess we forgot to mention that you'll be playing opposite Johnny Depp and Meryl Streep."

Joel adds his parting remark just loud enough for the rest of the Mafia to hear it. "Well, you'd better get your beauty sleep. You have a love scene tomorrow, and it's not with Meryl."

And as they walk out the door I turn to the Mafia and say, "Well, ladies, you heard the man. I've got to get my beauty sleep."

"JEW CAN'T JUS LEAVE!" the Don shouts.

And as I collect my things, I stop for a moment and look at them all, with their tight red dresses—some specially enhanced with a D cup too big for their frame, others with that perfectly frozen look that they have only achieved through a bucket of Botox—and I say, "You can keep my tips from tonight. I know you pocket some of them most nights for your bugger sugar, thinking I didn't notice. Anyway, I QUIT." And with that I walk out the door and into my future.

Okay, don't judge, it was a fantasy, and it helped me get through most nights in my own personal hell of cocktail waitressing. The reality, however, is drastically bleaker. There are no Coen brothers, no Johnny and Meryl, no pithy moments of lambasting the Cocktail Mafia . . . There is just me: injured, uninsured, and now jobless.

Gidget goes in for another bear hug before she departs. I manage to stop her at the pass and offer my hand. "Hoges . . . I gotta run to Barneys before work, but I'll see you soon."

And as she grasps my hand and almost shakes it out of the socket, I know I'll probably never see her again . . . and I'm okay with that.

The door slams, and I open the envelope. Three hundred fucking dollars? It was probably someone's birthday this week, but it sure as hell is not mine.

※※※※

Houston, we have a problem. I can't get off the toilet. Not in a Montezuma's revenge, trip to Mexico sort of way . . . I literally can't get off the toilet. I made this momentous discovery when I reached for the toilet paper on the wall in front of me. Just as I bent forward, my back seized. This is not a little pang, or a mere twinge; this is a "Holy shit, my back just pulled the emergency brake" moment. I'm really not sure how to deal with this situation. I am naked with my knickers around my ankles and my ass stuck on the porcelain goddess. It's not a pretty picture any way you cut it.

Okay, my options are:

1. I could yell for my neighbors. I live in New York and don't actually know most of my neighbors, and I'm not sure this would be the ideal way to introduce myself. Not an option.

2. I do, however, know the animals who live in the rent-controlled apartment above me, who have the charming habit of letting their shower or kitchen sink overflow, which causes it to rain in my apartment at least a few times a year. But after our last heated interaction (I guess "I am going to fucking kill you if this happens again" translates into Spanish . . . who knew?), I am quite sure they would gladly let me rot away on the toilet. Also not an option.

My phone starts ringing, about a mile away in my living room. Finally the answering machine picks up. "Hi, honey, it's Mom. Just seeing if you need anything after all?"

I find myself yelling toward the answering machine, as if by some miracle, she can hear me: "Mom, I'm stuck on the toilet and I can't get up!"

"Okay, Doll Face. I'll call you in an hour or so and make sure you're okay."

"I am not okay . . . I am stuck on the toilet," I bellow like a wounded animal.

And with the quick beep of the answering machine she is gone. Completely oblivious that her only daughter could possibly die on the toilet, which is a rather unglamorous way to go. I can hear the anchor now: "Ex-model-turned-actress lives through what should have been a fatal accident but is found dead on the crapper in the Lower East Side. News at eleven." I laugh at the thought, making things worse. The spasms are causing my body to seize in a jarring way that can only be compared to an earthquake in my nervous system. The toilet seat is cutting into my badly bruised rear end, my legs have lost feeling, and the only thing I can think of is that commercial from the nineties with the old lady who says, "Help, I've fallen and I can't get up."

An hour later, I'm still stuck on the toilet and my phone rings again. It's like Chinese water torture waiting for the answering machine to pick up. "Oh . . . hiya, Hogan . . . This is Andy . . . your EMT. I got your number from my ambulance report. And I was just wondering if you wanted to go out to dinner and drinks some time?"

I can't believe this guy.

"Anyway . . . it was nice getting to know you the other night. You seem like the quiet type . . . little quiet . . . which I like. And you were a very good patient. Did I happen to mention that you were a good patient? I thought your shirt that said 'Dump Him' across the front was real funny . . . ahhhh . . . anyway, my number is—" *BEEP.*

I would like to be dethroned now, like Mary, Queen of Scots. I am over this situation, and I am sick of staring at the photo across from the toilet of the little girl from Namibia who is mid-jump and laughing as her African village lies in the background. I used to love the photo because it seemed like she was laughing in the face of abject poverty . . . but on closer inspection over the last few hours I have become quite convinced she is laughing at me. Note to self: After burning the "Dump Him" shirt, take down picture of the little brat in the bathroom and install something useful like a rope so you can pull yourself off the damn john.

Hour three, and I am still on the toilet. "Hi, honey . . . It's Mom again. I am really starting to worry. If I don't hear from you in an hour, I'm going to call your brother to go over to your place and make sure you're okay."

"NO! NO! NO!" I wail as she hangs up. The only thing worse than dying like Elvis on the toilet is having your little brother come over and rescue your pantless self off the toilet.

"Come on, Hogan . . . you can do it . . . just get up," I repeat over and over again, like a drill sergeant. I put my right forearm down on the sink next to me and get a death grip with my right hand on the edge of the basin, slowly inching my left hand underneath my left butt check to make contact with the toilet seat. It will be a push from the left and a pull with the right. Considering that my arms are the only things working, I feel this might finally be the ticket. Yes, it is going to hurt like homemade sin, but my other options are dying on the toilet or having my brother come over. And once he gets a look at my sorry naked self on the toilet, he will be laughing so hard that I might need to rescue him from off the floor. And I can guarantee that if I ever get married, he will tell this story as the wedding toast. Avoiding that is motivation enough. One, two, three . . .

MOTHERFUCKER . . . OH SHIT . . . HOLY FUCK . . . (I think science has proven that if you swear when you are in excruciating pain, it helps the pain subside.) I am kind of up, well at least off the toilet seat. I slowly move my left hand to the towel rack in front of me with a death grip still on the sink. Eureka! I am up . . . in a ninety-year-old with osteoporosis way. But I am off the throne, and as God as my witness, I will never sit on another toilet again. I will pee standing up from now on.

〰〰〰〰

However, I discover there is a reason women sit down to go to the bathroom. I have now peed all over my toilet and the floor, and I can't get down to clean it up. My life has reached an all-time low. I think it might be time to go see a doctor, since it's been several days since the accident and I am not feeling any better, and I now have pee all over my bathroom.

I call to make the appointment. The receptionist answers the phone with the most annoying singsongy voice I have ever had the misfortune to hear. "Ortho-PEE-dics . . . Okay, let me get the appointment book. All right now, who is your health care provider? . . . Oh, I see."

The conversation pretty much goes downhill from there: "Well, are you on workmen's comp? . . . Were you hurt on the job? . . . A car hit you. Well, were you in a car? . . . No? . . . Well, that's no-fault . . . No, I'm not saying you were at fault. It's something that covers people hurt in car accidents, up to a certain amount of money . . . Well, you need to get a lawyer first and file all the papers before the doctor can see you . . . All right, well, give us a call back."

I can barely walk, and now I have to find a lawyer before I can see a doctor, to get something called no-fault, which will hopefully cover my medical expenses. I think I'm officially confused, and my life just seems to be getting more and more fun by the second. Thankfully, a bartender from work called me yesterday with the number of a personal injury attorney, just in case I need to lawyer up.

I have a car service pick me up at my apartment and drop me directly in front of the lawyer's building, because I am never crossing another street again, if I have my way. I hobble into the lawyer's office. He is a thin man and looks more like a choirboy than the pit-bull courtroom brawler that I was expecting. His perfectly manicured hands reek of privilege, and his limp handshake is reminiscent of a dead fish. The office is littered with huge files stacked on the floor. He tells me that each file is a different case, a different person. It doesn't really register that I, too, will be a file stacked on his floor. I sign papers, lots and lots of papers. He tells me what they are, but he talks so fast and I am in so much pain that I don't care if I'm signing away my first-born child at this point; I just want to get this done so I will be allowed to see a doctor.

It has been six days since the accident. My first appointment is with an orthopedist. I am shown to the waiting room, and after painfully getting into the chair, I look around the room. It is full of crippled people, in braces, with canes, in wheelchairs. I find myself staring, trying to figure out what had happened to them. I decide that the guy in the wheelchair with the cast on his arm and leg must have forgotten something very important when he jumped out of the plane . . . a parachute. The woman with the neck brace and badly bruised forehead dove into the pool, not knowing it was the shallow end. And the man with the leg brace, neck brace, and arm in a sling must have fallen down all twelve steps of AA. Okay, stop staring, read a magazine, I tell myself, as a little reminder that it is rude to gawk at the physically impaired.

I flip through the magazines: *Fitness*, *Muscle & Fitness*, *Shape*. Now, that is just cruel. What happened to *Highlights* magazine? Yes, it was boring, but it wasn't mean. This is a doctor's office for Christ's sake; can we have a little compassion for my fallen, clearly injured brothers and sisters?

Finally, I am called into Dr. McBones's office. "So tell me, how are you feeling? What pain are you having?" he says in the most professional of voices, to make up for the fact that he looks far too young, and is far too good-looking, to be a doctor.

"I can't sit, stand, or lie down comfortably. My back and neck are in constant pain, and it goes down my arms and legs. I can't put much pressure on my right knee without it giving way, and it sounds like grinding bones when I move it. I'm getting sharp pains in my head . . ." I pause in my grocery list of complaints; there is more, I know there is more . . . "Oh yeah, and I keep forgetting things. Like my mom's phone number, which she has had for the past fifteen years, or what I did yesterday, and I keep walking to the kitchen and opening the refrigerator, and I know what the refrigerator is, but I don't know why I am there or what I was looking for."

I am going to have to lie down on the table to be examined. My own personal Doogie Howser brings over a step stool to help me navigate my ascent. Once in a seated position, I decide to use a technique that I have developed in the privacy of my apartment to get into bed, which I have appropriately titled the Futon Maneuver. I extend my right arm out to get solid contact with the table, then I slowly lean to the right, placing my forearm down, and over I go to my side with a few grunts of agony. Once in a fetal position, I inch the soles of my feet flat on the table and slowly roll over onto my back. The whole process takes about five minutes and a variety of sound effects. I have never had an audience before, but I am quite sure that Dr. McBones is in awe of the Futon Maneuver.

The exam starts benignly enough, as he has me grab his finger and wiggle my toes. "Okay, I am going to move your leg now." He has barely moved my leg a few inches off the table when it sets off a chain reaction of spasms in my lower back that causes me to let out a scream that I'm sure is heard in Brooklyn. "Okay, okay, I'll stop," he says as he gently places my leg down and regains his hearing.

He hits my left leg with a little mallet to check my reflexes . . . and it moves.

He hits my right leg . . . and it barely moves.

He hits it again . . . and again it barely moves.

He looks puzzled. "Interesting," he murmurs in a contemplative way. "Well, we need to have you get MRIs of your back, neck, and knee, and then we'll have a better idea of why the right side of your body isn't responding. I want you to continue wearing your neck brace, but I also want you to wear this," he says, handing me a back brace.

I suddenly flash back to a modeling job I had in Paris. The rather malnourished and tragically fashionable stylist handed me a neck brace and chin strap ensemble, with a white button-down men's oversized shirt. "My agent told me I was wearing Gaultier clothes," I uttered in horror.

"Zese are Gaultier. It is ze, ow you say? Ze Wounded Wear," she replied with her pinched nose in the air, as if I had just committed the ultimate fashion crime.

I snap out of my memory just in time to grab the back brace

from Dr. McBones. "Oh, great. You know, I used to get paid to wear this stuff." As soon as I say it, I realize how it sounds. Oh my God, he thinks I'm an ex-dominatrix. He doesn't say anything, but from his beet red face and the nervous clearing of his throat, I know.

A rather pregnant silence ensues before Dr. McBones speaks again. "Okay . . . Well, I am also very concerned about your head . . . I mean your memory loss."

"Did I tell you that my head took out an entire windshield?"

"Yes, you did, three times, and you wrote it on your patient form," he responds in a worried manner.

"I did?" Crap, I thought I forgot to tell him, but I guess I told him and forgot.

"It's okay. I called a neurologist, and he can see you in an hour. You can pick up the prescriptions at the front desk, and I will see you back here in two weeks to go over your MRIs."

Needless to say I am taking a taxi to the neurologist's office. I never realized how bad the streets of New York really are. Every pothole is jarring my spine and making me yelp in pain. The braking is causing my body to thrust forward and rattle in the restraints of my neck and back brace. I am trying to fixate on the driver's taxi medallion ID on the plastic divider, as a way to take my mind off the pain. After my fourth yelp of agony from the backseat, my lovely cab driver, Mohammad Kabul license number 3469, turns around and catches a look at my Wounded Wear ensemble. "What happened to you?"

"I was hit by a car."

Mohammad sighs a bit and then sheepishly asks, "Was it a cab?"

I think Mohammad is truly concerned that *he* might have hit me, being that his driving skills resemble a bat out of hell. I decide to quell his fears. "No, it was a Mercedes."

"Oh, good for you, better than a cab."

The light changes to green, and off we go, me bouncing across the backseat in my Wounded Wear, and Mohammad rocking out to the top forty of the Middle East.

The neurologist, Dr. McBrain, resembles a walrus, and his monotone voice is lulling me to sleep until he takes out a shiny silver pin. "Now I am going to give you a nerve test. I am going to stick this pin in your arms and legs and test your nerves."

Come again? I am a patient, not a voodoo doll. He does my left side, and I definitely feel it. And then he does my right side . . . I can see the blood, but the feeling is dull. Dr. McBrain gets the same puzzled look that Dr. McBones had. "Interesting," he says, as if I am a mathematical equation. "I am going to have you go down the hall for a brain-wave test. I will see you in two weeks, and we'll go over your MRIs and tests. Pick up your prescriptions on the way out."

I limp down the hallway to my next chamber of torture. "Okay, mami, jew need to set in da chair." Juan, the brain-wave technician, then puts a white, Vaseline-like substance in my hair, and then gauze, and then attaches to my head all these wires that go to a large machine on a roll table behind me.

"Is this going to hurt?" I ask, worried because I have already shed blood at the hands of the voodoo-doctor/neurologist.

"No, mami . . . no pain, jew just set back and relax. Dis here machine sends message to jew're brain, and I record it."

After he removes the wires from my head, I ask him a very important question. "Do I look okay?" Probably a stupid question; I mean, how good are you really going to look in a neck and back brace? He does, however, assure me that I look presentable and even winks at me before I depart.

I go down on the street to catch a cab. It is rush hour on Thirty-fourth Street, and it is starting to rain. With no available taxis in sight, it is becoming apparent that I am going to have to take the subway, but the subway is across the street . . . and not just any street—this is the mother of all busy intersections, Thirty-fourth and Seventh Avenue.

I stand on the corner for ten minutes as cars zoom by and horns honk. I can't move; I am paralyzed with fear. The accident keeps playing over and over again in my head. I'm feeling nauseous and a little disoriented. I think I might be having a panic attack. I've never had one before, but I am quite sure this is what one feels like.

I spot an older woman in her seventies. I figure she will be my best bet for compassion. "Excuse me, ma'am. Do you think you could hold my hand while I cross the street?"

The words have barely exited my mouth when she bolts across the street, exclaiming, "What are you, some kind of weirdo?" It is clear that old doesn't necessarily mean kind, and that I am on my own.

"Come on, you can do it. The little man, that means walk. Don't look at the cars. Just focus on the little man," I say as I slowly inch out into the crosswalk. The hum of engines and the petrifying honking of horns is causing me to sweat like someone in the throes of menopause. "Come on, you're almost there . . . Keep going, keep going. YES! YOU MADE IT!"

Safely across the street, and rather impressed with my momentous achievement, I approach the subway entrance, and a woman moving at the speed of light barrels into me. "BITCH," I exclaim.

Then a man bumps me from the other side. "ASSHOLE," I blurt out before realizing that I probably resemble a Tourette's sufferer.

It takes me two hours to get downtown because I am moving so slowly. Limping into my apartment, I catch a glimpse of myself in the full-length mirror. Not only do I have on a neck and back brace, but my hair looks like I have cum matted in it, and it's standing straight up on end. The technician didn't even bother to take the gauze out.

———

I am still not quite sure what no-fault insurance is, and my lawyer can't seem to explain it to save his life, but through the little bit I can decipher from him and Google, I think I have a general idea. In the twelve states that actually have no-fault laws, if you are a pedestrian who is hit and injured by a car and the driver has insurance, no-fault (often referred to as Personal Injury Protection in auto insurance policies) helps you with your medical bills, regardless of whose fault said accident is (hence the name). You have thirty days in New York State to file a claim and send the no-fault application (form NF-2) to the driver's insurance company (which was one of the countless papers I must have signed at the lawyer's office). There are catches, though: In New York, no-fault only covers up to fifty thousand dollars of medical bills and prescriptions, and with the price of health care and the severity of my injuries, I could fly through that pretty fast, and that's the best-case scenario. Every month I have to be examined by a doctor who works for no-fault, and he writes a report, and some number cruncher behind a desk, who does not have an MD attached to his name, determines whether or not no-fault will still cover me. They can cut me off at anytime, regardless of whether or not I am still injured. For most people this is less of a worry, because if no-fault cuts them off, their normal health insurance will kick in and cover the rest of their medical bills. But for the uninsured—me—no-fault is all I have, which makes me feel about as secure as having a ticking time bomb on my jacked-up back.

I didn't have health insurance for the simple fact that I couldn't afford it, and now I get the sneaking suspicion that I am going to be paying for that for the rest of my life.

I have a major situation, apart from the obvious. I have no clean clothes, and the prospect of recycling dirty underwear out of the clothes hamper again is disgusting me. I try calling my brother to ask him if he can drop my laundry off at the wash-and-fold up the street. "No, I'm busy," he replies in a dismissive way.

"But, Spike, I have no clean clothes, and I obviously can't carry it myself."

"Well, I'm busy. Call one of your friends," he says, before hanging up on me.

What the hell is his problem? He's acting like he's mad at me, which makes no sense. I haven't done anything besides having the bad taste to get hit by a car. He saw the car. He was with me at the hospital. He even came over the next day with his two friends and brought me lunch, and they sat there staring at me as I tried to get down a few spoonfuls of lentil soup. You know what, I decide, screw him. I'm calling Mom and siccing her on him. She works guilt better than anyone on the planet, and her techniques are comparable to water boarding.

Yes, I am behaving like an eight-year-old tattletale, calling my mommy in California to rat out my adult brother, but he's behaving like a fucktard, and I need some clean clothes. Besides, he owes me huge for allowing him to live this long. Just for the record, when I chased him around the house with a sharp kitchen knife at the age of ten, I stopped myself before I drew blood, somehow knowing that prison was far worse than being grounded. And when I threw a kitchen chair at his head, at twelve, technically I missed; it merely grazed his arm. I will admit that pushing him out of the trapdoor of the playhouse, at six, where he dropped five feet and rolled about fifteen down the side of a hill, was not very nice, but we were playing war, and he needed to be sacrificed to the enemy. And at seven, when I jumped over five cacti on vacation in Arizona and then dared him to do it, knowing that he probably wouldn't make it, I have to say in my defense that I helped pick the forty needles out of his butt.

Besides these isolated incidents, I have been the picture of the loving and supportive sister. When he wanted to play dress-up or Barbies with me, I would let him. When he was scared of the dark, I would sleep in his room. (Or was it me who was scared of the dark? We'll call that one a draw.) When we were in high school and he had a bad mushroom trip and thought little purple men were chasing him, my best friend, Gayle, and I drove an hour to pick him up in a Safeway parking lot and only laughed at him twice. When he wanted to move to New York, I let him stay with me for a month, and he stayed for years. He is the worst roommate I have ever had, but I never kicked him out. When he slept with several of my girlfriends, and I would see them doing the walk of shame out of our apartment in the morning, I wouldn't chastise him; I would merely laugh. When he would sleep with underage supermodels, I would field the calls from their mothers wondering where their seventeen-year-old daughter was, and then gently tell my brother to get the jailbait cover of *Vogue* out of the place pronto. I have supported my brother on his successful life path to being a photographer-slash-metrosexual via Barbies and dress-up. I have saved him from rehab and jail. I put a roof over his head for longer than I care to admit. And thanks to my slutty friends, I got him laid more than most guys in New York ever dream of. In short, I am the perfect sister, and my saintly self needs some clean underwear ASAP.

I am reclining on my futon after calling my mother. It's getting a little exhausting trying to hide how truly injured I am every time I talk to her; I don't want her to panic any more than she already is. It was easy, ratting on my brother; not so easy, getting down on my futon. (Whose idea was it to have a futon? Oh, right, my bedroom by any other city's standards would technically be a closet.) Lying down is my only option after sitting was getting too painful. Plus, my Vicodin is about ready to kick me into a little nap. And then I remember: Just as the constant pain is my enemy, so is sleep, due to my recurring accident nightmares.

I am saved by the bell. Or should I say, the buzzer of my door. The ascension off the futon is a difficult and time-consuming endeavor. I roll over on to my left side and slowly inch my legs up into a fetal position. I stay in this position for a few seconds, taking deep breaths, before attempting the next move. Once I have worked up the momentum, I put my left palm down to anchor myself and slowly roll over to my stomach, with my bent legs still underneath me. This position is excruciating and must be abandoned immediately, which I do by raising myself up on all fours. I now slowly walk my hands up the wall . . .

BUZZ . . . BUZZ . . . BUZZ . . .

"Will you relax? I am moving as fast as I can!" I shout. Not that whoever it is can hear me down on the street.

Inch by inch, centimeter by centimeter, I work my way to a semistanding position. I stay here for a few seconds to make sure that I can feel my feet before I take my first step.

Next I must navigate down the four stairs from my bedroom. I have come to the conclusion that going down sideways is the best technique and puts the least amount of weight on my badly bruised right knee.

My feet hit the living room floor just as the buzzer goes off again. I stagger over to the intercom. "Who is it?" I ask, trying to conceal the fact that I believe him or her to be an impatient ass.

"Who do you think it is?" my brother curtly replies. Clearly my mother wasted no time.

I buzz him in and unlock the door. And what arrives is not my brother dressed in a shiny suit of armor here to save his sister and whisk her soiled laundry off to the Laundromat. What arrives is the wrath of hell. He slams the door behind him. His face is beet red, which only happens to his Irish mug when he has had a little bit too much whisky or when he is murder-you mad. Considering that it is only two thirty in the afternoon, I quickly deduce that it is the second scenario. He is doing his OCD pacing, but it is now accompanied by profuse sweating, and he is rubbing his forehead with the palm of his hand. In a nutshell, he is full-out postal.

"What are you, a fucking victim!" he shouts, with no question mark attached.

"What is your problem? I have no clean clothes!" I yell. I am trying to hold back the tears, but my usual wall of armor clearly got chinked in the accident.

"You know, there are two kinds of people in this world, victims and survivors. Are you a victim?"

"You know what? I am a fucking victim . . . I got hit by a car," I bellow. As soon as it exits my mouth I want to retract that sentence. *Victim* is not usually in my lexicon, and I am very uncomfortable using it to describe myself.

"I'm out of here. And by the way, it's New York, you can pay to have anything picked up or delivered to your house," he exclaims with a disgusted look on his red face as he slams the door.

I stand there stunned, looking at my dirty-laundry bag. I can't hold the tears back any longer. I am alone now . . . truly alone.

I don't understand why he's so angry. I mean sure, my brother and I fight occasionally, but this makes no sense. All our friends always comment on our closeness. We hang out all the time, go to the gym together, talk on the phone like gossipy schoolgirls, go out for drinks with our friends, and go to concerts together. He calls me for relationship advice or for my Martha expertise if he's in a quandary as to what to make for dinner. Any question he has I am basically his go-to girl.

My brother always says that he was raised by two women, my mother and me, even though I am only a little older than he is (we are what's known in Catholic circles as Irish twins), and I guess it's true. We were latchkey kids, and it was my job to make sure we came home from school together and did our homework. When he would get sick, I would stay home to take care of him. My mom depended on me. She had to work, and she didn't need to be worrying about what my brother was up to, which, at times, tended to the no-good category. He was, as my mom so eloquently put it, "all boy." After all, he was the inspiration for the "no cowboy boot" rule at nursery school, after he walked in and promptly kicked his teacher in the shin. And there was the time he came home drunk at the age of ten and announced that it was Jesse Jackson's birthday and he felt the need to celebrate. I threw him in a cold shower while he sang "Happy Birthday, Jesse Jackson," and my mom and I sat in the kitchen laughing like two adults as he puked in between verses. There was also the incident where he and a friend thought it would be a brilliant idea to shoot out all the windows of the Jehovah's Witness church with a BB gun, and let's just say a few Jehovahs witnessed it. Yes, the local police had our number on speed dial. None of this ever happened on my watch, though, because I knew better than to let him out of my sight for a minute.

On the opposite end of the spectrum was me. I didn't have the luxury of fucking up; I had a single mom, and I understood all that entailed. My mother couldn't be worrying about two children. So I got good grades, excelled at track and field, and didn't really get into trouble . . . I guess you could say I was a Goody Two-shoes.

The realization hits me like a ton of bricks. I have always been the strong one, the one he comes to for help or advice, the one he depends on . . . and now this. This accident has shaken a constant that he has had his entire life. He's angry because he's realized that I am not a superhero; I am not perfect. I am human. I don't know how to deal with this revelation, but I do know I can't lean on him right now. I am, however, going to need to turn to someone for support. Because I am afraid that I might be entering into the war of my life, and I might need a few people in my foxhole. I flip through my mental Rolodex, and I come up with three people. Three people who will not judge me, who will not view me as weak, or as a victim, who I hope will have my back no matter what. My mother and my two oldest friends, Mary Jane and Gayle . . . those are my few, my proud, my brave . . . Everybody else will get the CliffsNotes version because I'm not sure that they can handle the truth. And with that decision made, I Google "Laundromats that pick up and deliver" in my neighborhood. I find what I am looking for, the savior of my dirty undies, and I say right out loud, "I am not a fucking victim."

CHAPTER THREE

Marijuana Mama and Mary Jane

I am not allowing myself to be depressed, except for the first twenty minutes of every day. I have set my alarm clock to a Christian radio station; nothing like some good old-fashioned Bible thumping to shock my heathen heart awake. I press the snooze button and permit myself twenty minutes to have a full-on meltdown. This sends me down the slippery slope of existential inquiry . . .

Who am I?
What am I doing here?
Why is life so unfair?
Is there meaning in suffering?
Why am I even alive? I should be dead.
What is the meaning of life now?
Have I made a difference?

I don't have any answers, except for the last one, and the answer is no. No, I haven't made a difference; like Marlon said, "I coulda been a contender. I coulda been somebody." I just need more time.

Note to self: You will never tell a soul about these morning pity fiestas. They are pathetic and embarrassing.

Okay, I am now officially disgusted with myself and my waterworks festival. Time to start the day and get my sorry ass out of bed.

The Futon Maneuver is not working. Per procedure: I have rolled over to my left-hand side, slowly inched my legs up to the fetal position, put my left hand down to anchor myself . . . but in this position my back is saying, "Hell, no, sister. We won't go." It's comparable to a charley horse in my lower back, causing my butt to tense (like I try to do when I'm wearing a bikini), and I can't feel my right leg. I remain still, waiting to make another attempt at getting upright.

My bookshelf is staring at me: *Midnight's Children*, *Metropolitan Life*, *The Outsider* by Colin Wilson, Dostoevsky, McLuhan, Camus, Gide, Brecht, Nietzsche, *The Killer Inside Me*, and *Sex Tips for Straight Women from a Gay Man* . . . I thought I hid that!

Round Two is even more pathetic than Round One. My back pressed the abort button at the word *go*.

My phone is ringing. It sounds tragically close. I put my right hand down next to me and feel on the floor. Oh my God, someone is a genius, and that someone is me. I managed to bring my cordless phone into my bedroom last night before I went to bed. I don't remember doing it, but we'll worry about that later. I should contact Mensa immediately and inform them of my brilliance . . . but first I will answer the phone.

"Hello."

"Hi, honey, it's Mom. How are you feeling?"

"Oh, I can't get out of bed."

"I know the feeling. I had a horrible night's sleep. The damn cat was running laps in the bedroom last night, and it was really tough getting up this morning."

"No, Mom, I don't mean that figuratively. I literally can't get out of bed."

"Well, did you try walking your hands up the wall?"

"Mom, I can't get past the fetal position."

"Honey, I really wish you would just let me come and take care of you."

"I really don't think you flying from California is going to help my bedridden situation right now. I'm fine; I mean I am going to be fine once I get the hell off the futon."

"Well, I am going to call your brother."

"NO! The accident has completely freaked him out, and after the laundry incident . . ."

"God, I hate when he behaves like a little shit. Well, does Mary Jane have keys to your place?"

"Oh yeah, she does. She fish-sat for me the last time I went out of town. Way to save the day, Mom."

"See, Mommy knows best. You should also ask her to bring you some of her Jamaican healing herbs."

"Excuse me?" I ask, wondering if she has lost her command of the English language.

"Some pot, sweetie. I really think it would help those back spasms of yours. I've started taking a few hits off the peace pipe every night to help me with my tennis elbow and to help me sleep, and it's like magic. I am a huge fan. I might even start marching for marijuana for medicinal purposes."

"Oh my God, you're a stoner."

"I am not a stoner. I was out with my friend David a few months ago, and I was complaining that I couldn't sleep . . . and you know David's been sober for twenty years, but every night he takes a couple of hits off the peace pipe and sleeps like a baby. So I have been doing it, and it works, except when the cat acts up, so I think I might get her some of that catnip; they say it's like kitty pot."

"Well, Marijuana Mama, how's that sobriety thing working out for good old David?"

"Oh, stop. Now hang up the phone and call Mary Jane to help get you out of bed . . . and have her bring you some Jamaican healing herbs."

Just when I thought my life couldn't get any more *Twilight Zone*, my mother comes out of the closet as a stoner, and her pot dealer is a sixty-year-old gay man who's a member of AA.

I call Mary Jane, and she gladly agrees to come over and rescue my sorry self out of bed. She will stop over after she picks up her kids from school. I don't want to make a big deal out of the fact that it's three and a half hours until then. I hate to ask for help anyway, and she profusely apologized but is stuck at the DMV (and the New York DMV resembles the seventh circle of hell).

Mary Jane and I met on a modeling go-see (fashion speak for audition) in London. I had recently arrived from Milan, was renting a room in an English fashion stylist's apartment, and was desperately lonely. We struck up a conversation in the waiting room, discovered we were with the same agency, and decided to have lunch (shocking as it may seem, models do eat). Over the course of our lunch-slash-gabfest, Mary Jane bemoaned her living situation with the "Posh Chelsea girls," who were the biggest bitches she had ever met.

I told her that my flatmate was away and she was welcome to stay with me for a few days, as long as she didn't mind watching *Breakfast at Tiffany's* three times in a row, since that was my weekend plan.

"Oh my God. That's my favorite movie, too," she responded with glee.

It soon became clear that Mary Jane was the third member of my Holy Friendship Trinity, along with my mom and my best friend, Gayle. So at the end of the weekend I said to Mary Jane, "You don't need to go back with the posh Chelsea bitches. You're moving in here."

We were inseparable. We went on all of our appointments together. We booked jobs together. We dropped in to see our agents together (who started calling us "the twins"). We finished each other's sentences. We even found the same things funny, like the sign they would put up in the Underground if the subway was delayed: "Tube Delayed Due to Body on Tracks."

"Yeah, you can't really complain about that. Leave it to the English," we would laugh.

Then Mary Jane had the brilliant idea that we should go to Japan for a couple of months on modeling contracts. She had been there before and considered herself an expert on the country. I was sold on the idea after she told me that they throw oodles of money at American models (otherwise known as *gaijin fasshonmoderu*). "Come on, you're going to love it. It's the safest place in the world. You don't even need to lock your door. There is absolutely no crime. We're going to make tons of money, and did I tell you that the makeup artists give you a full facial massage before they apply your makeup?"

Japan is not actually in close proximity to the planet Mars, but I felt like I had landed there, only I was the alien. The billboards all moved, the taxicab doors shut by themselves, and the street signs were unreadable. The agency booked us into the Hotel Mental (seriously), and a padded room would have been a vast improvement over this place. It was situated right at Azabu-Juban, Roppongi crossing, which is the equivalent of having your bed in the middle of Times Square. The jet lag was kicking my butt in a big and major way; I was nodding off at castings and awake all night.

By day four I was over my jet lag and fast asleep when I was startled awake by footsteps. "Mary Jane, will you stop making noise," I growled, rolling over only to see Mary Jane asleep in her bed. "Oh my God! Mary Jane, wake up, somebody's in here!" I yelled, turning on the light, just in time to startle a Japanese man about to disrobe at the foot of our beds. At which point Mary Jane and I started yelling and screaming four-letter combinations that thankfully scared him.

"What room number?" he asked in broken English.

"Four-oh-two, motherfucker," I fired back.

"So sorry, four-oh-four," he eked out as he ran for the door. From then on we made sure to lock our door.

The work started pouring in, but it wasn't the types of jobs that I was used to in Milan or London. I unfortunately won the most ridiculous job competition when a makeup artist proceeded to put every color of the rainbow on my face, my hair in pigtails, and me into pink footed pajamas that zippered up the front. Just to add insult to injury, my direction consisted of the photographer laying down pictures from Italian *Vogue* and saying in broken

English, "Do these poses." After an hour I excused myself to go to the bathroom. The toilet was a high-tech computerized thing. I did my business, pushed what I thought was flush, and stood up to put my pink footed pajamas back on just as the toilet started erupting like Old Faithful, raining my own liquid waste all over my head. I walked back into the studio with a rainbow's worth of makeup dripping down my face. There was no explanation necessary, as the entire studio burst into laughter, each saying *"Kawaii"* (Japanese for "cute"), over and over again, as they pointed at me. I was not feeling very kawaii, but they simply dried me off, reapplied my makeup, and handed me a fresh pair of footed pajamas.

Mary Jane and I finally found a way to deal with the crazy world of the Tokyo fashion business: drinking. The one high point of living in the hotel was the close proximity to the clubs, where models drank for free. All the clubs were in one building, and we would work our way down the floors; by the time we got to the ground floor club we were usually pretty inebriated, but nothing compared to the Japanese businessmen we would see gathered in groups retching on the sidewalk. One particular evening Mary Jane and I crawled the two blocks to the hotel on our hands and knees. We simply reached our arms up, barely over the concierge desk, and they knew exactly who to hand the keys to. Needless to say, we weren't looking very pretty for the cameras the next day. We were, however, finally having fun in between our grueling work schedule, and soaking up as much liquor and culture as we could. We went to the temples and the public baths, where the Japanese have perfected bathing into a Zen-like art form. We also enjoyed grocery shopping and laughing over the astronomical prices.

"Hey, Hogan, let's get an apple. They're only eight dollars apiece," Mary Jane would mock.

"No. I've got a better idea. Let's get this bunch of grapes. They're on sale for a hundred and fifty dollars," I would snicker back before grabbing a bag of rice.

We arrived back in London to discover that our roommate, Dee, had been redecorating. She had moved her bed into the dining room, moved an Australian photographer into our room, and moved Mary Jane and me into her old room. It was a little confusing at first but a welcome surprise, since we now had a bigger room and two single beds. Mary Jane and I showered to get rid of the horrible film that seems to grow on your body after thirty-two hours of travel. We put on our pajamas and then greeted our new roommate.

"Hi, I'm Auss. I've heard a lot about the two of you from Dee. She did, however, forget to mention that you wear really un-sexy pajamas." Mary Jane and I looked down at our pj's. She had little polar bears on hers, and mine had little candy canes. We couldn't help but laugh . . . He was going to fit in just fine.

Mary Jane and I awoke the next morning and had a model meltdown. She had a cold sore, and I had a pimple the size of a small country on my cheek (obviously brought on by the long journey). Mary Jane decided that we should do a three-day fruit cleanse. She had read about it in some fashion magazine, and although it sounded horrible, it was less horrible than a cold sore and a pimple. By day three, we were bored and barely breathing. So we gladly accompanied Dee and Auss to the pub (it was, after all, Sunday, which in England is a pub-ly day of obligation). Mary Jane and I sat sipping water, as Dee and Auss downed a few pints.

Then Auss pointed out that English cider is technically fruit and would therefore qualify as part of our cleanse. It didn't really take much convincing. After two pints, and nothing but fruit for three days, we were drunk as skunks. In the morning, Mary Jane entered the bedroom in the same clothes she had on the night before, looking a bit worse for wear.

"Don't be mad . . . but I slept with Auss," she confessed, with a sheepish look on her face.

"Why would I be mad? I had the whole room to myself, although I was too drunk to notice. It's not like in Tokyo, when you slept with the hot Italian guy, and you left me with his ugly red-headed roommate . . . That was wrong."

Our days were filled with fashion, and our evenings were filled with Dee, Auss, and their friend Bud, who just appeared one night. I suspected that Bud was actually a piece of furniture, being that he rarely spoke and would just sit in the corner rolling joints. I was starting to get antsy, though . . . I think I was part gypsy at this point in my life.

"Let's go to Paris," I said to Mary Jane. "I've always wanted to live in Paris."

So off we went to Gay Paree, and as soon as we landed, I was in love. The Arc de Triomphe, the Champs-Elysées, the Louvre, the French women who could throw an outfit together like nothing I had ever seen before . . . it was all my wildest dreams come true. And then there were the cafes, in which we loved to while away the hours, sipping coffee and watching the Parisians go about their daily lives. On one particular Saturday, Mary Jane and I were sitting in a cafe in St. Germain when she asked me, "What is that guy doing over there, at that table?"

I turned around to look and observed a man in his thirties

seated at a table with two women and another man. One of the women had her arm across the table. "I think he's reading her palm," I replied.

We watched curiously as he read the woman's palm, and then the man and woman left, and he began reading the other lady. No money exchanged hands, which I found slightly odd.

"Let's go over there and see if he'll read our palms," Mary Jane cheerfully said.

"No way. That kind of stuff freaks me out. Besides, it's all phony; they just make stuff up. If he was really good, he'd be charging money," I retorted in a wearily dismissive manner.

"Well, will you at least come with me?" I acquiesced to accompany Mary Jane over to the table.

"Can you read my palm?" Mary Jane asked like a shy schoolgirl.

He gladly agreed, and we sat at the table, Mary Jane with her arm across the table, palm up, and me with my hands safely shoved under my legs on the chair. He told her that she either had just met or was about to meet her soul mate, and that this relationship would last forever. They would have three children, but her career wouldn't last very long.

"Would you like me to read your palm?" he asked me.

"No, thank you," I replied.

"May I just look? I won't tell you anything."

That seemed fair enough. I quickly wiped my moist palm on my pants leg and placed it across the table. He looked at it, and then he picked it up to get a closer look.

"No, this can't be," he said in a confused way.

"What?" I questioned, suddenly intrigued by the prospect of good news.

"I've only seen one other palm like this before, and that's my mentor's palm. See right here? This is your life line, and it just stops right here, but then next to it this line starts where the other one left off, but there is nothing connecting them," he said as he traced the lines on my palm with his finger.

"What does that mean?" I shrieked.

"Well, something is going to happen to you, and you should die, but you don't. It's a miracle that you live, and your life will be forever changed. It will be a rebirth."

"Great, she gets three kids and a soul mate, and I almost die?"

"No, you don't understand. This is so rare, it's a gift," he responded, still staring at my palm in amazement.

"But, when is this going to happen? What's going to happen to me? Can you tell me that?"

"No, I'm sorry, I can't. I can only tell you that it will happen, and just remember my words."

Two weeks later Mary Jane had to go back to London for a job, with the promise that she would return in a week, but a week came and went, and then another, and another. Finally, I got a message at my agency to call Mary Jane, with a telephone number that I didn't recognize.

"Where the hell are you? I thought you'd be back in a week," I asked.

"Sorry, but I got hit by a car," she responded.

"What do you mean you got hit by a car? Are you all right? Are you in the hospital? Do you need me to come take care of you?" I rattled with worry.

"No, I'm fine. The car wasn't going very fast, but I did get taken to the hospital. They checked me out, and I was just a bit banged up and sore. Did you know they don't charge you here for going to the hospital? I went to pay, and they said there was no charge, even for foreigners. Anyway, Bud took me to his place to take care of me, and now I'm living with him, and we're dating."

"Wait . . . you got hit by a car, and now you're dating the skinny English guy who used to sit in Dee's living room rolling joints?" I laughed, wondering if she had injured her brain.

"I know, right? Way to get a girl when she's down." Mary Jane snickered.

And get her, he did. Mary Jane came back to Paris a couple of times, but she had a LoJack on her for England—and Bud. I stayed in Paris for the next eight months, before the gypsy got the best of me again and I moved to Zurich and Vienna, before heading to New York. Mary Jane and Bud got married, and have been living in stoned bliss ever since. Thankfully, Bud's job forced them to move to New York a few years ago with their two little ankle biters, Peaches and Candy. Yes, they gave their little girls stripper names, in the contradictory hope that they'll turn out to be lawyers and doctors. I've met a few Chastitys in my life, and they were the biggest whores on the planet, so I think it might work out for them. God knows I could use a doctor in the family.

"We're here," Mary Jane calls as she opens my front door. Peaches and Candy tear up the four stairs to my bedroom, and plop down next to me on the bed.

"Hogan, are you going to get better?" Peaches asks.

"Does it hurt?" Candy chimes in as she hugs my teddy bear.

"Girls, treat Hogan like a china doll; she's really hurt," Mary Jane says as she stands in the doorway.

"How long have you been stuck in bed?" Peaches asks.

"The same amount of time you were at school," I reply.

"That's a long time. Did you have to go to the bathroom?" Peaches pries.

"Well, maybe you should wear diapers . . . I think they have them for adults. I saw a commercial once," Candy offers.

"Well, maybe you two should wear muzzles. I think they make them for kids," I retort, as they laugh.

"Ladies, why don't you go in the living room and play with Sushi, so your mom can get me out of bed."

"Can we put a mirror up to his bowl, so he'll fight himself?" Peaches asks.

"Sure, knock yourselves out. You can also feed him, since he's been on the Karen Carpenter diet since the accident."

"Why did you name your fish Sushi?" Candy inquires, even though she knows the answer and is just stalling in the hope of witnessing the pathetic sight of her mom pulling my sorry self out of bed.

"Because I'm a vegan, and I thought it was funny."

"Well, if you get any more pets, are you going to name them after food?"

"Yes, I'm planning on getting a potbellied pig named Bacon, a shar-pei named Raisin, and a golden retriever named after the Chinese dish of fried dog. Now, go play with Sushi, so I can get out of bed and make an appointment to get my tubes tied."

Mary Jane and I laugh as Candy exits the room to go torture my fish.

"Sorry about this. It's kind of friendship at its worst."

"Hey, that's what friends are for," Mary Jane reassures. "Now how should we do this?"

"Just grab my arms and pull me up, and no matter how much

I scream or swear, just keep pulling," I instruct. "Hey, girls, plug your ears because I'm probably going to be yelling four-letter words," I shout to the peanut gallery.

"It's okay, Hogan. We know them all from Mom," Peaches hollers back.

I shoot Mary Jane a look as she places on my dresser the joint that my Marijuana Mama insisted I ask her to bring. "Hey, I think I might nominate you for mother of the year," I tease as she gets into pulling position.

"Fuck off or I'll drop you," she says, chuckling.

"Hey, Mom, only Hogan can swear right now because she's hurt," Candy bellows from the living room.

"You heard the kid . . . now help me up, bitch." I laugh as she slowly grabs my arms and pulls me up to a seated position. We can't stop giggling, and I can't feel my legs, so we are going to rest in this position for a minute.

"Hey, when you got hit in London, what kind of car was it?" I quiz.

"A four-door black Mercedes . . . It's a little weird, isn't it? I wasn't hurt like you, though, and thank God I was in Europe, land of free health care," she answers.

"Do you remember that palm reader in Paris?" I ask.

"Oh my God . . . that's right. He told you that your life line was split in half. That something was going to happen to you, and you should die, but you don't, and it would change your life forever. Okay, that is fucking freaking me out."

"I know, I just remembered that today. I can't remember what happened yesterday, but I can remember stuff that happened years ago. By the way, you better take your birth control, because he told you that you would have three kids, not two," I bait.

"Shut up; I've got my hands full already. Now, let's get you all the way up," Mary Jane orders, grabbing my hands again.

The pain is revolutionary on my ascension, and with the number of four-letter words that I am able to cram into a few minutes, I think I might be eligible for the *Guinness Book of World Records*.

"Hey, girls, want to see what I get to wear?" I ask, once the pain recedes, putting on my neck and back braces.

"Cool! Do you get to wear those forever?" Peaches questions.

"Christ, I hope not. They don't really go with any of my clothes."

And as they depart, I quietly thank anyone who might be listening for a friend like Mary Jane, and I swear on a Bible and stick a needle in my eye that I will never tell Peaches and Candy what a slut their mommy was before she met their daddy. That's true friendship.

"Aloha, Mr. Hand." I am Spicoli stoned, or maybe I'm Slater stoned? "Behind every good man there is a woman, and that woman was Martha Washington, man, and every day George would come home, she would have a big fat bowl waiting for him." I don't know what it is that makes me quote *Fast Times at Ridgemont High* and *Dazed and Confused* every time I'm stoned.

I wonder if Mary Jane got her weed from another mother on the PTA? It's really strong: two hits and I am now officially the queen of Stoney Kingdom. Then again, I am not really an herbs woman; I don't think I've smoked weed in more than a year. My teeth feel like they have individual sweaters on them. Must have water, must get off the couch, but the couch is so comfortable, I am one with the couch. I could eat, I'm kind of hungry; no, it's just the munchies—you are not really hungry. I want to listen to the Grateful Dead right now . . . no, maybe Pink Floyd . . . no, Neil Young . . . I want to listen to Neil Young. This is really help-ing the pain. I move and a minute later I feel a muted pang or twinge, but I've already moved, so I'm over it . . . Awesome. Why don't doctors prescribe this instead of painkillers, muscle relaxers, and the anti-inflammatories that rip apart my stomach? I'm going to meditate on that, right after I get done thinking of famous stoners: Scooby-Doo, Thomas Jefferson, Willie Nelson, Snoop Dogg, Bill Clinton (you know he inhaled), Bob Marley, Jim Mor-rison, Sir Richard Branson, Shakespeare (he references it in son-nets 76 and 27), Stephen King, and George Washington. So that's three presidents, two dogs, a few musical legends, the greatest writer to ever live, the scariest writer to ever live, a billionaire, and let's not forget my latent pot-smoking mother.

Hi . . . I am high . . . Oh my God, I just had the most horrible thought . . . speaking of high, and things that are high . . . I might never be able to wear high heels again. This is a fate worse than death. I think I need to take all of my heels out of my closet and just say hello. They probably feel a little ignored recently, and I miss them terribly.

I am now surrounded by all of my exquisite heels on my bed-room floor. Oh, my Lanvins, crushed red velvet with a perfect red satin bow on the front. They are divine little works of art that make me feel like a 1950s I-like-to-have-tea-at-the-Plaza lady. My Marc Jacobs caramel brown soft leather boots that lace up the front. They make me feel sexy, bohemian, circa 1970s. My Prada black satin with ankle straps and delicate beading on the front. They say I am elegant, I am classy, and my legs look great. Black leather stiletto boots, same pair in brown (because I loved them so much), Dolce and Gabbana blue satin mules, Fendi black sling-backs . . . and so on . . . and so on. (I'm a New Yorker; I don't pay retail. All of these beautiful displays of femininity were purchased at either sample sales or consignment shops.)

The thought of spending the rest of my life in comfortable tennis shoes is not comforting at all; in fact, I can feel the waterworks coming on again. I am not a casual person; sneakers should only be worn to the gym or muddy sporting events. The only person who can pull off wearing sneakers every day is Ellen DeGeneres.

Sadly, my options are few, and my physical agony will not allow me anywhere near a heel of any kind. So, my beautiful ladies, I think I am going to have to cheat on you for a little while with that cad that hangs out in the corner of the closet, Adidas. They say the name stands for "all day I dream about sports," but I think it stands for "all day I dream about shoes" . . . real shoes with a heel. I promise to come and visit you once a week and tell you how much I love you, and hopefully someday soon I will slip you back on my nine-and-a-half narrows and you will make me feel like a woman again. Okay, I'm stoned . . . don't judge. Like my homey, Shakespeare, said, "To sleep, perchance to dream—ay, there's the rub."

CHAPTER FOUR

Sex: The Final Frontier

I wish I owned stock in the company that makes Post-it notes, because the wall above my kitchen table is covered with them. My reminders resemble those of a ninety-year-old with dementia: lock front door and put keys here (with an arrow pointing down to the table); orthopedist appointment Wednesday; neurologist appointment Thursday; go to police station and pick up accident report. I grab that last one and look at it closely. Oh, that's right: my lawyer told me that I need to get the police report of my accident and see if I can talk to the officer that came to the scene, in the hope that he will testify for me in court—I am suing the driver for damages. I asked him why he couldn't just have them mail it and call the cop himself, but he told me that cops don't like lawyers, so it would be better if I went. I'm not sure that I like lawyers, either, since this will involve me gimping twelve blocks there and twelve blocks back, as cabs are not in my dwindling survival budget. When getting from the bedroom to the kitchen is the equivalent of doing a triathlon, twelve blocks is like walking to China. It is, however, good to have goals to break up the monotony of convalescence . . . so the police station will be my goal.

First, I must pick out an outfit. I decide on a brown mod wool dress, black tights, and motorcycle boots. The dress says, I am a fashionable, law-obeying citizen, and the motorcycle boots say, I am a local East Village resident who refuses to wear tennis shoes. It's a cute look until I put on my neck and back brace. I don't care how skinny you are, a back brace just makes you look fat. I wear it over my clothes so it's very obvious I am injured. The neck brace, however, is impossible to work with, and gives the appearance that I have more chins than a Chinese phone book. A little lipstick and blush is just the thing to put the zing back in my pale and drawn complexion; just as Holly Golightly said in *Breakfast at Tiffany's*, "I've got to do something about the way I look; I mean, a girl just can't go to Sing Sing with a green face."

Time to review Post-its again: *Don't leave house without keys, wallet, and cell phone (arrow pointing down to table)*. Yes, I am *Memento* girl. I still have my sense of humor, though—I also have a Post-it that reads, *Don't forget, you're a sexy bitch.*

And I'm off . . . moving at a turtle's pace. I don't walk anymore; I shuffle. I haven't even made it a block and a seventy-year-old Hispanic man who passed me a minute ago is now three blocks ahead of me. Show-off.

Block two seems like an extraordinarily long block, and it is becoming rapidly apparent that motorcycle boots were a bad idea. I need to take a rest; I lean on a building and take a few deep breaths.

"You okay, lady?" a young guy asks, as he walks out of the braiding/barber shop.

"Yeah, I'm fine," I respond through clenched teeth.

"You don't look too fine. I mean you look good, but what happened to you?" he asks, gesturing to my neck and back brace.

"Oh, I'm just a fashion victim . . . No, I'm kidding. I got hit by a car."

"Oh man. Was it a cab? Those drivers are mad crazy," he says, as he rearranges his baseball cap.

"No, it wasn't a cab."

"Damn, that's some wack shit. Well, I'm gonna keep an eye out for you. I work at this here establishment. I'm Miles."

I extend my hand. "Nice to meet you, Miles. I've got to run, I mean limp, to the police station now. I should be back by Christmas, so buy me something nice."

"You funny. I seen you around before, but now I'm gonna say hi. Dat okay?"

"Of course, Miles. It would be my honor. I'm sorry, did I even tell you my name?" I ask, before releasing my grip on the building to shuffle away.

"No, but I'm just gonna call you Gap Girl, cuz you look like a Gap ad."

I chuckle as I wave good-bye. I know he just paid me a huge compliment in his mind, but I don't own one article of clothing from the Gap, and the only ad I resemble right now is one for a short school bus.

It's block five, and I am praying for death and taking another brief rest while clutching the rim of a garbage can. By block eleven, I am ready to make a sign, put out a cup, and call the nearest doorway home. A few weeks ago I was in peak physical condition, going on four-mile runs across the Brooklyn Bridge before working out at the gym for two hours, five to six days a week, and now I can't even walk a block without taking a rest.

Finally, I arrive at the police station. I walk up to the front desk and tell the female officer that I would like my accident report. I give her my name, the date of the accident, and the location. She finds it and as she grasps it in her official hands, she asks, "How would you like to pay for it, check or money order? It's ten dollars."

"Well, I can pay with cash or credit card," I respond.

"We only accept money orders or checks," she says in a clipped judicial tone.

"But I don't have my checkbook, and I don't know where to get a money order. Besides, everybody takes cash."

"The New York City Police Department doesn't. There is a place four blocks down that has money orders," she fires back.

"But you don't understand, it just took me over an hour to walk twelve blocks. As I'm sure you've noticed, I am in a neck and back brace, which obviously means I am injured, and my accident report that you are holding confirms that I was hit by a car. Can I please just pay in cash?" I plead.

"Sorry, we don't accept cash or credit cards. We only accept checks and money orders; it's procedure."

New York City's finest has me so angry that I am ready to kick kittens. "I hate her" is my mantra for the next forty-five minutes that it takes me to hobble four blocks to get the money order and four blocks back. The pain has me in tears by the time I reenter the police station. There is now a male officer standing behind the desk with Officer Bitch.

"Are you okay?" he asks. "Did someone hurt you?"

I point at the woman. "She made me walk four blocks to get a money order to pay for my accident report."

He turns to the female officer. "Why didn't you just give her the accident report? I mean, look at the poor girl."

"We only accept money orders and checks; it's procedure," she responds like Robocop.

"Sorry about her," he says to me with a comforting smile as she walks away.

His name is O'Leary. He's brought me over a seat, to wait for O'Connor (the officer listed on my accident report), who should be arriving to work any minute. "So with a last name like Gorman, you gotta be Irish, right?" O'Leary, with a face that has the map of Ireland all over it, makes small talk.

"Well, my grandfather was a football star at Notre Dame, and my mom is an ex-nun, so I think that officially makes me Irish royalty, in a princess of potatoes sort of way."

"Yeah, that's pretty Irish. I'm Irish, too," he states.

"Well, with a name like O'Leary, I figured you probably weren't Polish."

O'Connor approaches. Thankfully, Officer O'Bitch has disappeared, because I am sure this is breaking her precious protocol. I explain why I am there. He has a quizzical look on his face as he looks over my accident report. "Oh, wait, I remember you now. I didn't recognize you at first."

"Yeah, I probably look a little different than I did when I was lying on the pavement surrounded by a windshield's worth of shattered glass. Now I have a shattered body and a couple of braces."

"You're lucky to be alive. I go to accident scenes all the time, and when we rolled up to that one, I was positive that it was a fatality. Those people that hit you were real jerks, I remember that.

Yeah, if you need me to testify, just have your lawyer call me,"
O'Connor says as he pats me on the shoulder and walks away to
clock in for work.

"Come on, Gorman, my partner and I will drive you home,"
O'Leary instructs as he escorts me out of the building.

I never thought I would be glad to ride in the back of a police
car, but the idea of traveling twelve blocks home on foot has me
thrilled to ride criminal-style. Just for the record, I did not ask
them to turn on the siren—they offered.

They just slid me into the metal cocoon, and it is rapidly becoming apparent that MRIs are not the ideal procedure for someone
with claustrophobia. It is the equivalent of being in a mechanical
coffin, and the loud noises it is making are not doing much to
subdue my fears of impending radioactive doom. I must stay perfectly still for the next hour, which is not only difficult in my
present physical condition but also going to make the panic attack
that is creeping up on me a bit of a bitch. This is the first of three
MRIs that I will have today (neck, back, right knee), so I will
spend a total of more than three hours in this device of taphe-
phobia torture. I have always had a fear of being buried alive
thanks to Edgar Allan Poe and his graphic descriptions in "The
Premature Burial," which Alice Anne Baybore insisted on reading
to me at the age of eight, in a pitch-black house, by candlelight,
for extra dramatic effect. She was a dark little girl, in a Tim Burton–
in-training sort of a way, and her delivery was so creepy that I wet
my pants that night and acquired a new lifelong irrational phobia.
I wonder what ever happened to that bad little seed? She's proba-

bly a mortician or haunting houses somewhere, while I am being buried alive in an MRI machine.

Okay, I need to think of calm thoughts. The ocean is a good one. The sound of the waves, the smell of the salt air . . . wait, scratch that. The ocean will make me think of water, and water will make me think of peeing, and I can't move for the next hour.

Note to self: Drinking a large bottle of agua this morning was probably not the smartest idea.

It's amazing how slowly time passes when you have nothing to do in a metal tube. It runs a close second to taking a long car trip when you're a kid, and the minute you pull out of the driveway you instantly have to go to the bathroom, and feel the need to ask every five minutes, "Are we there yet?" Let this be a lesson that MRIs and car trips with children should be avoided at all costs in the future.

Speaking of costs and things that are costly, I am starting to worry about money, so let's take this time in the mechanical coffin to go over the present scenario I find myself in. I don't have a job anymore, and quite frankly, with the amount of pain I am in, I can't work anyway; they don't seem to be paying people these days to lie around and moan in agony. Which means that money is flowing out, but no money is flowing in. I have a little bit of savings, and if I give up things like taxicabs, eating, and breathing, I can probably survive for a couple of months with the help of my credit card. "There are some things money can't buy. For everything else there's MasterCard." No-Fault is supposed to reimburse me for prescriptions, which it looks like from my last trip to the pharmacy are going to run me three hundred dollars a month, so if I charge the prescriptions, then I can use the check No-Fault sends me toward bills. I'm not exactly Suze Orman, but whatever, at least I have a plan, and if by some unfortunate turn of events my money and credit run out before I get better, then I'll know where to come to be buried alive. Like the Poe who gave me my fear in the first place said, "I have great faith in fools; self-confidence my friends call it." Or maybe it's "Once upon a midnight dreary, while I pondered weak and weary."

Oh, Edgar Allan Poe . . . I hate you sooooo much right now.

After a few days of driving myself crazy, wondering what my MRIs will show and if I have permanent damage to my brain, I have decided to focus on the bigger question: Will I ever be able to have sex again? I am a girl who has always enjoyed sex. Not in a slutty, I'll-fuck-a-stranger-in-a-bar-bathroom sort of way; but if I'm dating someone, I would have sex twenty-four hours a day if I could. I only started dating "Brooklyn" (guess where he's from) a couple of weeks before the accident, and we have not actually technically sealed the deal. He's come to visit me a few times and brought me homemade CDs with titles on them like "The Music You Can't Remember Since the Accident" or "Songs to Sing When You're Road Kill." We clearly have the same taste in music and sense of humor. He is an adorable tortured boy in corduroys, which is totally my type.

Anyway, he's coming over tonight for a visit. I've put on a little makeup and lightly glossed my lips for that subtle kissable quality. I am wearing my favorite blue vintage T-shirt (which brings out my blue eyes) and snug-fitting jeans (which accentuate my butt). This outfit says, "I don't need to try too hard . . . but I still look sexy." Unfortunately, my neck and back brace are messing up the look a little, but the back brace does make my 34Cs look huge. I have dimmed the lights for that romantic mood, Nina Simone is playing softly on the stereo, and I have a bottle of Pinot and two glasses set out on the table. I think about lighting some candles but decide it would be overkill. I'm kind of impressed with my Martha-like ability to create ambiance.

I shuffle over to the door and let him in, thinking, God, he looks cute. We exchange an awkward hug and then I pour us some wine, and we sit on the couch.

"So, what have you been doing?" he asks. I don't want to tell him that I've mostly just been making the five-foot journey from the bedroom to the living room a few times, and that my big achievement for the day was taking a bath, although it took me forty-five minutes to get out of the tub because my leg went numb. Or that I am getting these piercing pains in my head, as if someone were repeatedly stabbing me, which are accompanied by loss of vision, and if they happen while I'm standing, I'll fall over. Nobody wants to hear you complain except your doctors. It's boring, and it's definitely not sexy.

I finally answer his question, "I haven't really been doing anything." And then I pause and strike the sexiest position I can muster in a neck and back brace as I cut to the chase. "You want to make out?" I ask, giving my best come-hither bedroom eyes.

"Are you sure? I mean you look great . . . I just don't want to hurt you," he states, moving closer to me on the couch and putting his arm around my shoulder.

"How much worse could you hurt me?" I just want to be touched, and touch, and feel sexy and normal for a second. We walk into my room. Well, actually, he walks and I hobble, after I take off my neck and back brace in the living room. Keeping them on might ruin the mood. He undresses me slowly, as if he's undressing a china doll. As he takes off my shirt he caresses my breast, and I almost orgasm just from that. Don't judge—it's been awhile.

Ahhhh . . . kissing . . . kissing . . . and more kissing. Forget meds and doctors, this is what I needed: some old-school Marvin Gaye sexual healing. I decide to take it up a notch and give him a hand job. I'm quite good at them. He is upright and accounted for in a matter of seconds. Things are right on track . . . and then . . . I can't move. I can't feel my right arm. Christ, I can't feel my left arm either.

I look down to see my frozen hand wrapped around his dick in a way that you see people with cerebral palsy hold their hands. A look of confusion crosses his face. "Why did you stop, Hogan? What's going on?" He looks down and assesses the delicate situation.

I immediately burst into tears. "What the hell is happening to my body? I can't move my arms," I wail.

He cautiously removes my hand from his family jewels. I continue crying as he sits there watching me and massages my arms and hands for the next twenty minutes until I finally get the feeling back.

"You okay now?" he asks.

"Yeah, I'm fine." I'm not fine at all. He knows it and I know it. But it's easier to lie than admit how scared, not to mention how embarrassed, I am.

He leans down and kisses me on the forehead, like you kiss a sick child when you don't want to catch what they have. "I've got to get to work, but I'll call you tomorrow."

"Sure, we'll go dancing," I say, forcing out a laugh and holding back a tear. I know he'll never call. Hell, I'd run, too, if I were him. Unfortunately I can't; this is now my life.

After Brooklyn says his last good-bye and walks out the door, I put on three things: my neck brace, my back brace, and "Songs to Sing When You're Road Kill." And as the first song plays, every lyric seems like Bob Dylan is singing just for me and quietly cutting me to the bone: "Once upon a time you dressed so fine . . ." I play this one song over and over again, and I cry—for the life I am living, and the one I have been forced to leave behind. I don't know who I am anymore. All the labels I have firmly attached to my ego are now gone: I am not an actor now (they usually like actors to be able to move and remember lines); I am not athletic now (I can barely walk a block); I am not intelligent now (I have always prided myself on having a mind like a steel trap, but that's gone); I am not a waitress now, or even employed (I've had a job since I was nine years old); I am not fun now (because nothing is fun about this); I am not even a sexual being now. What does that leave me with? I don't know. I don't know anything, except that I need my mom. I dry my tears and try to regain semicomposure as I pick up the phone and dial.

"Hi, Mom?" I ask before I realize that the person on the other end of the phone is speaking Spanish, and the last time I checked, my mother was not Latin. "Oh, I'm sorry; I must have the wrong number," I apologize before hanging up the phone. I am pathetic. I can't even remember my mother's number.

I look up my mother's number in my address book and take three deep breaths, knowing that this will be the hardest phone call I'll ever have to make, and probably the most selfish thing I have ever done in my life.

"Hi, Mom . . . no, I'm fine." Get back in there, tears. "I

mean . . . I really hate to ask, but I'm not doing so good. Do you think you could come . . . just for a week?" Abort, abort, meltdown approaching. "Thanks, Mom . . . I love you, too."

My mom likes to say that when I was born the doctor brought me to her, and as she held me in her arms for the first time, she looked at me and said, "I don't know what I am going to do with you, but we are going to be best friends." She was right on both counts. She didn't have a clue what to do with me. She ordered a fancy diaper service but had never heard of diaper pins, so my diapers were tied on me until one of her friends enlightened her when I was a month old. But we were best friends, and I was her confidante even before I could talk. My brother was born a little over a year later. I was the result of a hole poked in her diaphragm, and my brother was an "Oh-I-just-won't-take-my-birth-control" baby. She wanted children more than anything, so she just made sure she got them.

My parents' marriage was over when I was eight. My mother, my brother, and I crammed ourselves in the front seat of the Audi, with all our belongings in the backseat and nowhere to go. She found a low-income-housing building and sat on the front steps of the management office every day for a month, until they finally gave her an apartment. With a place to call home, she then had to figure out how she was going to support us. She was beautifully trained to do nothing, being an ex-nun-slash-stewardess. (She became a nun to rebel against her parents; of course, most people at the time rebelled by taking acid and chasing a rock band around the country, but not my mom. She decided to really piss her parents off and chase Jesus into a convent. When she left the convent, she became a stewardess, because that's what all ex-nuns do. So, really, if you think about it, she was the flying nun and clearly had a thing for uniforms.) But she wasn't going to let a little thing like lack of experience stand in her way, so she rented a typewriter, taught herself how to type, and took any job she could get . . . a bakery, a moving company, a tree experts company, a hospital administration office, a law office.

For two years after the divorce, my brother and I ate hot dogs and mac and cheese for dinner every night. It was economical and, frankly, pure heaven for us kids. But Friday night was our big night out: pizza night. One Friday my mom came home and announced that there would be no pizza night because she had no money. My brother immediately burst into tears. "But it's a tradition," he wailed in the Elmer Fudd way he used to talk. So Mom and I started flipping over cushions and emptying out pockets looking for change, and we managed to pay for pizza and a salad bar with ten dollars and twenty-five cents in coins. My brother stopped crying, tradition was not broken, and all was right with the world again.

My mother never pretended to have all the answers, and her only rule was, "Don't lie to me. No matter what you do, I will back you up as long as you tell me the truth." So I told her everything, and she would listen intently and offer advice if needed, but never judgment. My friends were always envious. They lived in big fancy houses with all the accoutrements money could buy, but they always wanted to hang out in our tiny apartment because I had something they didn't have: a mother who they could talk to.

We faced some tough times, but we faced them together, and we had something that money couldn't buy: love. Most kids my age didn't know what they wanted to do in the future, but I knew exactly what I wanted to do: I wanted to go off and make my fortune so that I could support this woman, who had given so much to me, so she would never have to worry about money again. I wasn't supposed to get hit by a car. This wasn't part of my master plan, and now I'm calling her to come take care of me, just like I never wanted to have to ask her to do again.

CHAPTER FIVE

As If Being a Blonde Isn't Challenging Enough

"Oh, sweetheart, I am so glad to finally be here," my mother says as she stands in my doorway. "My driver, Ali, is bringing up my suitcase." My mother always manages to rope cab drivers into carrying up her suitcase to my apartment (which is unheard of in New York). And sure enough, within a minute Ali arrives, suitcase in hand.

"How do you do that?" I ask with a laugh.

"Well, I spent the entire ride from the airport telling him about your accident, and then I told him that if I hurt myself carrying my heavy bag, I wouldn't be able to care for my injured daughter."

"Guilt . . . the Jews own it, but the Catholics rent it." I giggle and shake my head.

"So true, now give me a hug," she says with a smile. Her hugs are legendary. She holds you close, and with the palm of her right hand she makes a circle twice on your back followed up with two little pats, and those tiny, perfectly timed gestures give you an instant infusion of love and a sense of security that can only be described as feeling like home. "Crap . . . I promised myself I wouldn't cry. I'm just so happy that you're alive. I don't know what I'd do without you," she says as she releases the embrace. "You look good."

"Liar," I respond.

"Well, I've seen you look more attractive, but alive is a hell of a lot better than the alternative."

She then proceeds to give me a blow-by-blow account of her journey from California to New York via Chicago. Starting with getting up at o'dark thirty, her super shuttle to the airport with the "slowest goddamn driver on the planet," and of course the people she sat next to on the plane. She feels that it is her civic duty to learn the life stories of anyone seated next to her. The woman would have a conversation with a doorknob given the opportunity, and the doorknob would end up adoring her and confessing to her its lifelong battle with its backstabbing friend Key. My mother is like Annie Hall all grown up, so much so that anytime I see Diane Keaton interviewed I can't help but feel that she and my mom were somehow separated at birth. I've never been happier to see anyone in my life and simultaneously felt so horrible, knowing the sacrifices that she has made to get here.

"Why don't you go put on your pajamas, Doll Face, and I'll get out your little gifts."

"Mom, you didn't need to bring me anything."

"Oh, stop. Go get into comfy clothes and let me play Mom for a minute."

I go up to my bedroom, take my pajamas out of my drawer, and then it all goes tragically wrong.

"Hogan . . . honey . . . are you okay?" my mother bellows from the living room.

"Yes, I'm fine," I squeak out, trying to hide the pain.

She scurries up the four stairs to my bedroom and finds me flat on my face. "Jesus Christ! You just fell over like a tree!" she screams. "Is this happening a lot, sweetheart?" she asks as she helps me up off the floor.

"Yes. I don't know what's wrong with me. I get these stabbing pains in my head, and then my vision goes, like when you stare at a lightbulb too long and all you can see are blurry dots, and then I lose my balance because my legs are always numb."

She guides me into the living room and pulls out a chair for me to sit in, and then she sits across the table from me. The worry on her face is palpable. "That scared the hell out of me. Not exactly what a mother wants to see . . . her baby doing a face-plant on the floor. I just want to kill those people that hit you. My athletic daughter who goes to the gym six days a week now has trouble walking across the room." She is swallowing her tears and trying to regain semicomposure. "I'm sorry . . . it just makes me so angry. It's easier when things happen to me, but when things happen to you, I'm supposed to be able to fix it. That's what mothers do."

"I am going to be fine," I state, trying to quell her fears. It's not a lie per se; it's more of a mantra. I am hoping that if I keep saying it, my body will follow suit.

"You know what we need? A little chardonnay therapy. Sometimes things don't seem as bad after a glass of wine, and it might help those back spasms."

Vicodin and wine . . . Mother knows best.

"Your orthopedist is cute," my mother loudly whispers as Dr. Mc-Bones walks out of the examining room to get my MRIs. She is right . . . Dr. McBones *is* cute, in a hot MD way . . . or is it just that I haven't gotten any since Brooklyn took off? My mother and I rarely agree on the definition of cute in the male department (she likes the collegiate, intellectual types, and I like the shy, starving-artist types), but Dr. McBones is somewhere in the middle of both our versions of male perfection. He's kind of Hugh Granty, minus the English accent.

He reenters the examining room and places my MRIs on the light board, and as he tells me the results, I can't help but imagine what he would look like naked.

"You have herniations of the lumbar spine at L4–L5 and L5–S1," he says, pointing to the damaged discs on the MRI. "And herniations of the cervical spine at C6–C7, C2–C3, and C3–C4." Oh, that is sexy. I love the way he points and uses big SAT words all at the same time. "Now, your herniations press on nerves, which is causing the numbness in your arms and legs. You have tears to the two main ligaments in your right knee, the ACL and meniscus . . ." Tears? I'd like to tear that shirt right off him. "We can start physical therapy and hopefully that will help your knee for the time being . . . Hogan, are you listening to me?"

"Yes, doctor," I respond with a flushed face, jarred out of my own personal skin flick.

"Now, I want you to see this neurosurgeon and have him look at your MRIs," he says, handing me a card. "And here is a list of physical therapists. You should start PT as soon as possible."

"Let's get physical . . . physical . . . I want to get physical," I say in a pathetic attempt to be witty, Olivia Newton John–style. Which sends him on to his next patient rather rapidly.

My mother rolls her eyes. "You are such a dork."

It's a well-known fact that everything I know about flirting I learned in the third grade. I have absolutely no game; I just geek out. But there is always the next visit, where I am sure to make Dr. McBones fall head over stethoscope.

At my next appointment, Dr. McBrain informs me that the brain-wave test shows that my brain is slow in responding and extremely swollen. It can take anywhere from six months to a year and a half for the swelling to go down and for them to determine whether there is any permanent damage. As if being a blonde isn't challenging enough.

With all this rather bleak news, my mother and I have decided to do what we always do when life gets too much to handle: we are going to the movies. Our record is three movies in one day, right after my grandmother kicked the proverbial bucket. There is something about the darkness of the movie theater, the stories, and the actors on-screen that magically make your problems disappear as you are whisked off to an imaginary world. That's why I wanted to be an actor in the first place, so I could do for other people what so many actors have done for me over the years.

We usually deliberate over what movie to see, but considering the circumstances, it's my call, and I feel *Eternal Sunshine of the Spotless Mind* is the only appropriate choice.

"Hogan, honey, I think you should sit here," my mother says, pointing to the handicap seat at the back of the theater.

"I think you should shut up," I reply with a laugh.

"I'm not kidding. You can't sit for two hours, and in this seat you can stand up when you need to, and there is also room for you to stretch your leg out."

"I hate you," I retort, knowing that she is right.

And as the lights go down, and I settle into my special-needs seat, I am magically whisked away to a world where everyone's lost their memory.

My mother and I have developed a routine to deal with our least favorite part of the day—morning. We grunt at each other for a few minutes, and then I go take a shower, and she heads to Starbucks to get her latte and my grande soy, no water, no foam, Tazo chai. This morning is no different; my mother is en route, dressed like she is on a day pass from the Bellevue psych ward. She insists on wearing her pajamas underneath her raincoat, and when I comment on her attire and express concern over the fact that a cop might mistake her for a crazy homeless person, she responds, "Well, sweetheart, I have my sunglasses on, and nobody can see me."

Yes, it's worrisome on several different levels. It is, however, less worrisome than the fact that I have just fallen while getting out of the shower.

"I'm back!" my mother hollers, as she opens my front door.

"I'll be right out," I answer. I read somewhere that one-quarter of the bones in your body are in your feet. In which case I can't feel one-quarter of my bones, and the rest are in excruciating pain as I slowly pull myself up. I will not be telling her about this because she will insist that I get a handicap railing in my shower, or something equally offensive.

"The funniest thing just happened," my mom says as I exit the bathroom.

"What? The fashion police gave you a ticket for wearing your pajamas in public?"

"No, I was on my way to Starbucks, and this young guy starts yelling, 'Yo, lady. Yo, lady.' Of course I don't think he's talking to me, so I keep walking. Then he shouts again, 'Yo, lady, are you Gap Girl's mom? I mean, are you the blonde's mom?' So I turn around, and he says, 'You're walking the wrong way to get your coffee.' And he walked me all the way there. Isn't that sweet? I used to worry that your neighborhood was a little dangerous, but it's nice to know that people look out for you in such a big city."

———

Dr. McSurgeon examines my MRIs with a look that is somewhere between shock and ecstasy. His skin is shiny, like it's made out of plastic, and his hair doesn't move even when he turns his head. Is he a doctor or a cartoon character? It's a bird, it's a plane—no, it's plastic man.

"Well, at least I didn't break my back," I state, trying to defuse the situation in a glass-half-full way.

"Actually, a break would be easier. You have five herniated discs between your cervical and lumbar. Most people come to me with one herniation, in excruciating pain, and they require surgery," he responds, in a dry, matter-of-fact tone.

"Surgery?" I nervously ask.

"Well, what I would do is go in and take out the matter that is pressing on your nerves. For your neck, I would go in through the front, move aside your larynx and vocal cords, and repair the damage," he states, as he aggressively demonstrates slicing the air with his pen. Oh my God, this is Looney Tunes.

My mother gasps.

"Mom, relax, just breathe," I coach.

"I'm sorry, it just sounds horrible." She quivers.

Dr. McSurgeon continues to describe his Jack-the-Ripper tendencies. "For your back, I would make an incision down your spinal column and remove the matter. It's not a one hundred percent fix, but it could give you relief and more mobility. Now, the risk is that we take out some of the cushion between your discs. So over time your discs could fuse together by themselves, which would leave you with no mobility." Maybe that's what happened to his hair? It lost mobility.

My mother gasps again, and Dr. McSurgeon's habit of air slicing is not helping my anxiety level either. This guy wants to filet me like a side of beef.

"Call me crazy, but those odds don't sound too good," I counter.

"Nobody is cutting on my baby's back," my mom adds.

"Well, you do have another option . . . epidural steroid injections. Some people get relief from those," he says somewhat petulantly, like a little boy who just had his favorite toy taken away. I don't bother to ask for details. Whatever they are, they sound a lot better than surgery. After watching this guy slice the air with his pen, I can only imagine what he would do to my poor spine.

"I think I should change my ticket, so I can be with you when you get the procedure done," my mom says as we walk out of Dr. McSurgeon's office.

"I'll be okay . . . It's only a little injection. How bad could it be?" She's already been here a week, and while I'll hate to see her go tomorrow, I can't, with a clear conscience, let her stay any longer. Every day she is here she's missing work, and when you live paycheck to paycheck, it's as if I am taking money out of her already empty pocket.

I have been to see the pain management doctor, and he gave me a nerve root block shot, which has done nothing to alleviate the pain, so we are moving forward to the epidural steroid injections that will hopefully be the salvation from my constant agony. The receptionist informed me that they will not perform the procedure unless I have someone accompany me and have a ride home, because "Your legs won't be working very well, and you'll be unsteady." I didn't have the heart to tell her that my legs don't work very well these days, anyway, and I am prone to doing face-plants into the floor. Mary Jane—the only person I know in New York who has a car—has kindly offered to drive my sorry ass to the office in Brooklyn. (Although Brooklyn is only across a bridge, I am always a bit disappointed that I don't get my passport stamped when I cross over, as it feels to me like another country, where they speak this strange language called Hipster.)

Upon arriving at the car lot where Mary Jane parks her car, we are met with a rather delicate situation: the gate is padlocked, the attendant-slash-owner Jose is nowhere to be seen, and there is a U.S. marshal standing in the center of the lot looking very official.

"Excuse me," Mary Jane shouts to the marshal. "I need to get my car."

"I'm sorry, ma'am, I can't let you do that. These cars are being impounded."

"What do you mean 'impounded'?" Mary Jane's voice raises an octave higher. "I pay to park my fucking car here."

"Ma'am, this is an illegal parking lot. The man that was charging you doesn't actually own this property. It is a vacant lot owned by a real estate developer, and Mr. Sanchez took it upon himself to trespass and start charging people money."

"Well, how the fuck was I supposed to know that?" Mary Jane hammers. Her face has now turned a fire-engine shade of red.

"Well, did you pay him in cash, ma'am?" the marshal questions.

Mary Jane takes this as a personal attack on her moral fiber, and just like the Pentagon pushed the injured Jessica Lynch to the forefront to try to justify its presence in Iraq, Mary Jane has slightly pushed me forward. "I have to drive my friend who got run over by a car to the doctor, where she is getting a shot the size of your forearm shoved up her spine. Have you ever seen an epidural, sir?"

"No, ma'am, I can't say I have, but—"

"Well, I have, and I opted for natural childbirth after getting a look at the size of the needle, and the video they show you of epidurals gone wrong—"

"Ma'am, I need you to calm down."

"Where the people are left completely paralyzed with spinal fluid leaking out of their backs."

I'm not really sure whom she is trying to scare right now? But from the look on the marshal's face, I think she has accomplished scaring the shit out of both of us. I have never seen Mary Jane get mad like this. She's one of the mellowest people I know, but I am a bit worried that she might start spitting green pea soup in a second.

"Mary Jane, breathe," I instruct, before turning my attention to Mr. Official. "Sir, I'm really sorry, I know you're just doing your job. My friend had no idea that this was an illegal parking lot; she's from California and very trusting. We really do have to get to the doctor, so if we could please just get the car back?" I plead.

And by some miracle, I have brought peace to the Middle East, and we are safely in Mary Jane's car and off to another country called Brooklyn. Her car is like a portable petri dish, with empty soda cans, kiddy books, discarded candy wrappers, and a fur coat's worth of dog hair, but I am used to it, since she is not much of a housekeeper either.

"I thought you were going to have an aneurysm back there. Did Bud decide that you both need to quit smoking pot again?" I question. Mary Jane and Bud have two fights a year, and I can practically set my watch by them. Fight one happens right before they go on vacation in August, and fight two is when Bud decides once a year that he is quitting smoking weed, which means Mary Jane, as the supportive wife, has to quit as well. It never lasts more than two weeks, but it is the longest two weeks of my year while they both go a little insane. And whenever they have their bi-yearly blowouts they both talk to me, because I'm neutral like Switzerland.

"Yes, I am going to fucking kill him," she fires back.

"No, you can't kill him, and you can't divorce him, because you two are my only model of matrimonial bliss, and somehow it gives me hope that maybe someday I'll find someone stupid enough to want to spend the rest of his life with me. Besides, his sobriety only lasts a couple of weeks. So you'll be back in stony bliss, when?"

"Christ . . . I can't take another week of this," she responds with a laugh. "His mood swings are a nightmare."

"Okay, Mother Teresa, just for the record, you almost verbally castrated a U.S. marshal back there. So when you were talking about the epidurals gone wrong, and the size of the needle, were you just exaggerating due to lack of THC?"

"No," she responds.

"Well, you could have lied to me and told me it was like a pinprick."

"You're my best friend, I can't lie to you. That's what friends are for . . . the truth, like you just told me I'm acting like a bitch. And the truth is, the only prick in this equation is my husband."

Wow, that is truly amazing, the way she just wrapped that back around to her domestic dispute. Speaking of wrapping around, we have just circled the same nine-block radius eight times, looking for a parking space.

"I fucking hate Brooklyn Heights. You have about as much chance of winning the lottery as you do finding a parking space here."

And just as she says that, we find a spot, eight blocks away. And I am hoping that maybe, just maybe, Dr. McPain has an IV bag full of medical marijuana for Mary Jane and a very small needle for me.

Being in a waiting room with a bunch of people in pain is about as fun as hanging out in a mortuary. Actually, the dead don't complain or take deep breaths and sigh every time they move, hoping that you'll ask them what's wrong—and even if they could, it's pretty obvious what's wrong with a dead person. As I quietly judge this party that I don't want to be at, I realize that I am on the guest list when the receptionist calls my name and hands me some papers to read and sign.

"Hey, Mary Jane . . . Want to hear the side effects?" I ask, deciding to get the party started right and entertain the room. "The risks of this procedure include a worsening of your pain, bruising, infection, epidural hematoma, headache, hypertension, difficulty breathing, numbness of extremities, possible allergic reaction, pain at the needle site and in nerve root distribution, stroke, permanent numbness, permanent weakness, permanent fecal incontinence, permanent paralysis, permanent urinary incontinence, permanent sexual dysfunction, or death. Christ, if you can't shit, can't pee, and you can't have sex for the rest of your life, death would be a welcome side effect."

"Actually I think *incontinence* means that you can't control yourself, so you shit your pants," Mary Jane says with an informative air.

"Wow, that's sexy. You'd still be my friend, right?" I laugh.

"Yes . . . but I'm not changing your diapers." She giggles.

The rest of the waiting room is not at all amused; in fact, they are shifting and deep breathing more than ever.

"Hogan, the doctor is ready for you," the nurse calls out.

And with that I am escorted to the VIP section, otherwise known as the very sterile surgical room.

"The doctor will be with you shortly," the nurse says, leaving me in the room by my lonesome.

When they say "the doctor is ready for you" or "the doctor will be with you shortly," I am coming to realize that it, in fact, means "I am taking you to purgatory, where you will wait some more in a cold and antiseptic environment, and have ample time to replay horrible scenarios of impending doom, over and over in your head, before this country's version of God decides to grace you with his white-coat presence." And this doctor is indeed my god right now, because he might be the one to get me out of the hell of my constant pain. Minus the possible side effects of shitting my pants, never being able to have sex, or dying, I am hopeful that these injections will be my salvation.

Dr. McPain enters the room in a rather rapid fashion, only twenty minutes behind schedule. He is a wiry little guy who I suspect used to be a bit larger. He wears his gym clothes under his white coat, has a high-pitched voice, and seems like he's had one espresso shot too many . . . I wonder when Richard Simmons started moonlighting.

Within a matter of seconds, I am facedown on a surgical table, with my bare ass in the air. "Now, I am going to insert this epidural needle through your tailbone, up into your lower back. Then I am going to take two other needles with steroids and put those into your lower back. You must stay perfectly still during this procedure, because if the epidural is placed wrong, it could cause paralysis," he says, as he prepares my injections and his assistant efficiently wipes my butt with antiseptic. He then rams the epidural in, and I finally understand the true meaning of pain. It feels like I'm getting gangbanged by a needle the size of a Mack truck.

"OH . . . SHIT . . . OHHH FUCK . . . MOTHERFUCKER . . . OHHH!" I scream.

"You're doing great . . . just keep still," he coaches, as he rams it up even farther. He's clearly said this same phrase hundreds of times before.

"WHAT PART OF 'SHIT MOTHERFUCKER' MEANS I'M DOING GREAT? THIS IS LIKE HAVING A TWO-BY-

FOUR SHOVED UP YOUR ASS . . . OHHH!" I bellow, praying for the side effect of death.

"Well, the guy before you almost broke the table, and then he fainted."

"WELL, THAT OUGHT TO TELL YOU SOMETHING!"

CHAPTER SIX

This Is My Pee Cup

You know those moments in life when you realize that a relationship is just not working out? Your calls go unreturned for days, you feel that he doesn't take you seriously, and he treats you like you are insignificant? Any person worth her salt would break up with someone who did that. So I am dumping my lawyer.

It has been months since the accident, and he has still not contacted my only eyewitness.

He has forcibly suggested, several times, that I have surgery on my neck and back. When I said that the only way I would have anybody carve on my spine was if I could find a neurosurgeon with minimally invasive techniques who wouldn't butcher me and possibly leave me worse off, like Dr. McSurgeon seems to be proposing, he laughed at me and stated, "A leading neurosurgeon wouldn't touch you with a ten-foot pole. You have no insurance, no money, and the only doctors that will see you take no-fault insurance. Top surgeons operate on the rich, not charity cases." In short, he is lacking a sensitivity chip and not really doing his job.

So while I might not be able to have the leading neurosurgeon in New York, I can sure as hell have the best personal injury attorney, but how does one find out who that is? I mean, sure, there are those commercials with really unattractive middle-aged men telling you that if you have been hurt in an accident to call them at 1-800-Ambulance-Chasers. But even I know that the best personal injury lawyers are too busy defending the injured to put on powder and prance around a TV studio.

My accident made one thing very clear: When something devastating happens, you really find out who has your back. A lot of people run away because either they don't want to deal with your drama or it makes them question their own mortality. Others stay by your side through thick and thin because they just love you that much. And then there are the people who run toward you as if *lured* by the drama—better to focus on someone else's disasters rather than their own. That person right now would be Posey, and as I discuss my dilemma with her, quite frankly I am glad for her interest, whatever her reasons for it. "This is ridiculous; you need a new lawyer. I'm calling my father's entertainment lawyer and finding out who the best personal injury lawyer in New York is, and I'm setting you up an appointment," she says in a take-charge way.

Posey and I are more acquaintances than friends. In fact, she kind of pisses me off even on a good day. She is beautiful—she looks like Elizabeth Hurley, if Elizabeth had one too many cream puffs. She's also a walking encyclopedia, but she always has to be right, and she's talented enough that if she'd ever bother to go on an audition she'd work nonstop, but her one tragic flaw (as she sees it) is that she was born to an incredibly famous father. She has massive "Daddy didn't buy me a pony" issues. If she could get her life together she could rule the world, but instead she is a Buddhist and a champion of endangered dolphins one week, a Kabbalah devotee and rain-forest advocate the next. This week I am her rain forest, which is kind of appropriate since I am prone to falling over like a tree, and her mission in life is to find me the best legal representation before she charges on to Scientology and saving the whales.

"Okay, you have an appointment tomorrow at twelve with the best personal injury firm in the city. I just emailed you the info," she says, before launching into a painstakingly detailed description of the hoops she had to jump through with Daddy dearest's staff to land this information. I know exactly where this monologue usually ends up, and listen intently to the trials and tribulations of being born with a silver spoon up her ass, because she just did me a huge solid, and I will be eternally grateful. I am biting my tongue so hard that I am sure to draw blood.

I am early for my appointment at the law firm of Advocate, Legal Eagle, and Solicitor, and I have just made a horrible discovery: Their office is a block away from Century 21, the Mecca of designer discount shopping. I have thirty minutes to kill (as a Virgo, I am eternally early). I'll just take a quick browse. No harm can come of that, right? BA (before accident), I was a firm believer that when the going gets tough, the tough indulge in a little retail therapy.

Nothing like a new dress to turn your frown upside down. Times have changed, and retail therapy is not an option, but looking is free, and I'm all about free-.99 these days.

I am clearly a glutton for punishment, and just to make matters worse they are having a sale. A Miu Miu dress for eighty dollars? This is torture. I am like a diabetic in Magnolia Bakery, salivating over all the delicious designer desserts. Oh, Dolce chocolate brown pants . . . you are decadent. Champagne-colored Armani dress . . . you are delectable. Jimmy Choo . . . I want you. The ring of the registers as women pay for their fashionable finds is giving me vertigo. I feel a little dizzy with envy. I just caught myself fondling a Dries van Noten jacket like a Catholic priest after Sunday school. My evil twin is saying, "Come on, just get one little thing to make yourself feel better." My good and practical twin says, "No. Your bank account is seconds away from nonexistent, and you are living off your credit card. Clothes are not part of the survival program. Walk toward the light, the light is good . . ." For one brief moment, I actually contemplate pulling a Winona Ryder, until reason rescues me from Kleptomaniaville.

I shoplifted designer jeans at the age of eleven from a store whose owner was a friend of my mom's (clearly I was not a criminal mastermind). I made a clean getaway, but I confessed to my mother the next day with trembling lips. She did what any parent trying to teach her child values would do: She marched me right into that store and made me hand over the goods and apologize. I will never forget the look in the owner's eyes as she said, "I expected more from you. I thought you were an extraordinary child, but you are just common." That day I made a vow to never behave in a common way and to strive to be extraordinary. My mother decided that was sufficient punishment, but I begged to differ and grounded myself for a month.

So come on, extraordinary child, walk the hell out of the store. You might be empty-handed, but class can't be bought or stolen. Besides, Marc Jacobs wouldn't design your trial wardrobe.

~~~~~

I am a little nervous sitting on the carved wooden chair in Advocate's office. The framed law degrees on the wall scream, "I am important!" and he looks the part with his perfectly coiffed white hair and green cashmere sweater. There is an air of confidence about him that one only acquires when he knows he is the best, and it is apparent that I am not interviewing him; he is interviewing me. Legal Eagle, a very tall man (who makes me look like a midget at five-foot-ten), has a sturdy build, and in his suit, sitting on the couch taking detailed notes, he looks more like a firefighter than a lawyer. Solicitor is lean with a runner's body and an animated face. He is pacing the room, rubbing his chin, and throwing in his two cents here and there. It is reminiscent of the Spanish Inquisition.

I give them the details of the accident. "The people who hit me replaced the windshield of their car without informing their insurance company, but it's written on the police report," I say, handing Advocate the document across the table. "And here are my MRI reports."

I can tell that they are impressed with the deteriorative state of what used to be my spinal column, right knee, and brain. I feel like I am waiting to get picked for the kickball team in the third grade . . . please pick me . . . please be my lawyers . . . please . . . please help me. Because personal injury lawyers work on contingency, taking one-third of your settlement as compensation, they only take on cases that they think they can win.

"I see here on your emergency room report that you told them that you had surgery on your knee at thirteen. Why did you tell them that? It was so long ago," Advocate questions.

"Well, because it was the truth. They asked me if I had ever had surgery before," I answer earnestly. Shit. Did I just ruin my only shot with the best lawyers in New York with my honesty policy? Don't they believe in that swearing to tell the truth, the whole truth, and nothing but the truth stuff, or is that just on TV?

Advocate and Legal Eagle chuckle a little. "Good answer. I think you have an excellent case. The vehicle was going at an uncontrollable speed down a one-way street. Your head shattered an entire windshield, and the eyewitness account of the accident on the police report matches yours. I can tell by the way you sit in a chair, and the way you walk, how injured you are. Which the jury will see as well, and that will make you a good witness on the stand," Advocate states.

"Does that mean you'll represent me?"

"Yes," Advocate answers with a smile.

"Well, which one of you will be my lawyer?"

"We will all be your lawyers, but we each specialize in different areas of the case. He will be your go-to guy," Advocate says, pointing to Legal Eagle. "So any question you might have, he will be here for you."

And just like that, I have a new legal team and my very own go-to guy. I feel better already; this seems like the first piece of good luck I've had since hitting that windshield. I want to jump for joy and yell, GO TEAM, but I think I better wait until the ink is dry on the contract. I can't wait to tell my old lawyer to suck it.

I received an email a few days ago that a friend is organizing a girls' clothes swap, where you can either trade your clothes with other women or sell your clothes. Yes, it has come to this. I think I've been in a state of denial about my financial situation, but I can't ignore it anymore. Yesterday I had to pay for my groceries in change, much to the annoyance of the cashier. My rent was due on the first, and it's now the seventeenth, and my landlord is only going to believe I'm on vacation in Jamaica for so long. My credit card statements resemble the debt of a small country, and I had to use the last of my savings to pay the minimum so that I don't ruin my credit. No-Fault is supposed to give me lost-earnings reimbursement, since I am too injured to work, but because my last waitressing job had rather creative accounting techniques, my old pay stubs only show minimum wage and not all the tips I made, so No-Fault only gives me a few hundred dollars every few months, which doesn't even put a dent in my overhead.

In a nutshell, I am screwed, and now I am going to have to sell some of my clothes in a last-ditch effort to survive. The selection process was a little *Sophie's Choice*, and although I didn't speak in a Polish accent, I did cry a lot as I cleared out half my closet. And now here I sit in the plush showroom of the hostess with my clothes meticulously laid out on a table and priced to perfection. The other women seem gleeful with the prospect of revamping their wardrobes, and I am miserable at the thought of parting with some of my favorite pieces.

"Oh, Prada. I need to try these on," a trophy-wife-looking woman says, grabbing a pair of my pants off the table. She slides them on and sucks in her stomach as she zips them up.

"Those look great on you," her mousy friend exclaims. Actually they don't look that great on her, and they're causing some camel toe action, but I am not here to judge, I am here to sell.

"I love them," she states before turning her attention to me. "Can you come down on the price? Forty dollars is a little high."

"They're Prada," I retort, in a bitch-you-must-be-high-if-you-think-forty-dollars-is-too-pricey way.

"Oh, I don't know, then. My husband has me on a budget, and I just bought a Kelly bag last week."

I can't believe she is trying to bargain me down, when she just spent more on a purse than some cars cost. "Fine, thirty five," I say, remembering that I have bills to pay. I'm sure the camel toe will go great with her Hermès bag.

My wardrobe is proving to be very popular with the others, as they circle and sniff around my designer duds. I have already sold quite a few pieces, but right now I secretly want to rip my vintage Diane von Furstenberg wrap dress off the woman who's trying it on. I am having purger's remorse. Hopefully, she won't want it, and I can covertly slip it back into my bag.

"Love it. I'm gonna take this dress, the Marc Jacobs shirt, the Anna Sui dress, and the Armani pants."

So much for hoping. I think Buddhists believe that you shouldn't be attached to material possessions, so maybe this is a sign that I should never become a Buddhist, because this is killing me.

"Hogan, can I talk to you?" the hostess, who is as cute as a cupcake, asks in a hushed tone.

"Yeah, what's up?"

"Well, this is supposed to be a clothes swap, and you haven't bought a single thing, or even traded any of your clothes. You're just selling."

"Oh . . . I don't really need anything. I'm trying to be more Buddhist these days."

"Well, it's rude. You should walk around and at least buy something," she says in a snitty Miss Manners sort of a way, while she teeters on her Christian Louboutins.

Under any other circumstances, I would agree that maybe I am not being a team player, but this is a little more than spring cleaning for me, and the only team that is going to pay my bills is my team of one. But she doesn't know about my financial ruin—nobody does—and I'd like to keep it that way.

"Sorry, my back is just killing me, but I'll look around now," I say as I make a move to view the others' clothes. Normally, I love to shop, but this isn't shopping; this is a hunt to find the cheapest thing I can. Finally I spot a no-name wool jacket for twenty dollars. I don't even bother to try it on, but it looks like it will keep me warm if I become homeless, which is an imminent possibility. Even though I've made three hundred and fifty dollars today, I'm still miles away from paying my bills.

⌁⌁⌁⌁⌁

It's been about a month since my last epidural steroid injection. I have had several over the past few months, and let me tell you, they haven't gotten any easier. They also haven't given me any relief. I am at home playing my new favorite game, "What doctor appointments do I have this week?" (with more doctors than an eighty-year-old, physical therapy twice a week, and going to no-fault doctors once a month so they can determine whether they will still cover my medical expenses, my calendar reads like *TV Guide* during medical disasters week), when all of a sudden . . . I am sweating, I feel nauseous, and the left side of my back feels like someone is kicking it in with a combat boot. As you can imagine, I am no stranger to pain by now, but this is different. Primal moans are coming out of me, and I have turned into Pukeahontas, hugging the porcelain goddess like a college kid on spring break. Of course, I think I have a medical license now because I spend so much time in doctors' offices. I diagnose myself with stomach flu, which is causing my back to spasm out of control.

By day two, the pain is unrelenting, my face is a sallow green color, and the only thing I can keep down is water. I try to duct-tape a bag of frozen peas to my lower back in an attempt to stop the tenacious kicking sensation, but it does nothing except remove the top layer of my skin when I tear off the tape. The only thing that seems to subdue the pain for a few minutes is a warm bath. I sit in the tub until the water turns cold and the torment returns. I'm afraid that this is probably not the stomach flu, and I don't know what to do. I have no insurance and no money, but I think I might be dying. Maybe if I call Dr. McPain, he'll be able to help me.

"Hello, Hogan. What seems to be the problem?" Dr. McPain asks.

"Something is really wrong. I've been projectile vomiting for two days, and the left side of my back feels like I'm being punched by a heavyweight boxer. It's the worst pain I have ever felt in my life," I moan.

"Well, why are you calling me?"

"Because you are my pain management doctor, and I'm in pain?"

"I can't really tell you what's wrong with you. You should

probably go to the emergency room," he instructs in a dismissive manner.

"I can't go to the emergency room. I have no health insurance," I whimper, before hanging up the phone.

Day three, and I am doubled over on my living room floor moaning, "Oh stop . . . please . . . stop."

I guess my moans are loud because one of my neighbors is knocking on my door. "Are jew okay in dere? Jew know if he hits jew once, he'll hit jew again. Dis has been goin on for three days. Jew should really call da police."

"Stomach flu," I bellow back, until she finally walks away.

I have promised my mother that if I don't feel better by tomorrow I will go to the cheap health clinic near my house. She wanted me to go to the emergency room, but after the way I was treated post–car accident, I am afraid that they will just turn me away.

Day four: I have been in the packed waiting room of the clinic for three hours. When one feels as bad as I do, things like image and decorum go out the window. So I have lain down on the dirty floor in the fetal position, among the seated ill and injured of New York.

"Hogan Gorman, the doctor is ready for you," the nurse calls.

Of course the doctor is not really ready for me, and I have to wait even longer in the exam room, but I am getting closer to diagnosis or death, whichever comes first. When the doctor finally enters the exam room, I'm pretty sure he's accompanied by a choir of angels. He takes my blood pressure, my temperature (which is high), and then has me give him a urine sample.

"Miss Gorman, there is a shuttle bus leaving for the hospital in fifteen minutes. You need to get to the emergency room immediately; you are urinating blood," he says urgently.

"But I can't go to the hospital . . . I have no insurance. That's why I just waited three hours to see you," I cry.

"Miss Gorman, we're not equipped to deal with what's wrong with you here. You need to go to the emergency room. Get on the shuttle bus."

The wheels on the bus go round and round,
round and round, round and round.
The wheels on the bus go round and round,
all through New York.
The pain in my back goes pound, pound, pound;
Pound, pound, pound;
Pound, pound, pound.
The pain in my back goes pound, pound, pound,
all through New York.
My stomach on the bus goes yack, yack, yack;
Yack, yack, yack;
Yack, yack, yack.
My stomach on the bus goes yack, yack, yack,
all through New York.

I am delirious from the pain, rewriting children's songs in my head, and the guy across the aisle from me looks to be carrying the tip of his finger in a Ziploc bag with ice, which is not helping my nausea. Several children are crying in unison as an elderly man coughs into a bloodied handkerchief, and we are all joined together by one common denominator on the express bus to hell: We are sick or injured, we are uninsured, and we are scared.

My cell phone is ringing. It's my brother. I don't really feel like talking, but I should let someone know that I am on my way to the emergency room, and give him a heads-up that he might be an only child soon. As I hear him say hello, I burst into tears.

"Hogan, what's the matter? Where are you?"

"I just want to die," I eke out through my tears.

"Don't say that," he says, trying to calm me down. "What's happened?"

I give him the highlights of peeing blood, projectile vomiting, and the horrible pain in my back that has me praying for death.

"Shit, dude. I'm stuck on a photo shoot all the way upstate. Call me as soon as you get out of the hospital, and have them give you that stuff that stops you from throwing up."

Of all my symptoms, the vomiting has him the most worried. My brother and I share a horrible fear of throwing up, which stems from one awful summer during our childhood spent at a Catholic Youth Organization camp. A company donated English muffins to the camp, so it was English muffin French toast for breakfast, sandwiches on English muffins for lunch, and hamburgers on English muffin buns for dinner. By day two most of the camp had food poisoning so badly that each cabin had a garbage can in the center for a communal vomitorium. That day my brother came up to me crying in the cafeteria, homesick and terrified of the plague that had struck the camp. "Hoge, I don't want to throw up," he cried. And I was right there with him, after hearing the horrible retching all night, but I had to pull my eight-year-old self together and reassure my little brother. "Just stay away from the English muffins. Eat anything but the English muffins, and you won't get sick," I instructed. Turned out that I was right, and my brother and I were the only two campers not to get food poisoning, but we were forever scarred. That's probably why to this day I get very religious when I'm praying to the porcelain goddess, in an "Oh no, God, please not again, God, oh God, please make this stop" sort of way. Although right now puking is running a close third on my list of phobias, behind peeing blood and the horrible sucker punches in my lower back.

———————

In the hospital admissions office I faint from the pain, I think right before the nurse was going to ask me who my insurance provider is. They throw me on a gurney and take me back to the ER.

The emergency room is crowded, with doctors in scrubs bustling around and tending to the ill. The elderly woman in the bed next to me is being questioned by a doctor.

"Ma'am, do you know what day it is?" he asks.

"Of course I do, it's Thursday," she answers with authority. (It's Tuesday.)

"And who is the president?"

"Roosevelt."

I want to tell her that Post-its are the perfect aid to a brain injury or dementia, but I'm preoccupied with my own agony and moaning like a porn star.

"Okay, little lady, I'm going to give you something for the pain," the doctor says, as he sticks an IV in my arm. And within a few minutes, I meet my new best friend: M-O-R-P-H-I-N-E. All of a sudden the pain is gone, and I am swimming in a drug-induced euphoria. I like this stuff . . . No, it's bigger than like . . . It's love . . . It's definitely love. I love it as much as I loved unicorns as a kid. *Unicorn* is a funny word, isn't it? And it's making me think of corn, which is the only food that looks the same way going in as it does coming out. Nobody really talks about it, but it is one of the most confounding mysteries of the universe. I wish I could listen to some music right now . . . David Bowie . . . I want to listen to Bowie because I am floating in a tin can in a ground control to Major Tom sort of a way, and I like it. I am perfectly content to lie on this gurney for the rest of my life, although I wish I had a stuffed animal to curl up with because I'm feeling a little womblike. When my brother was little he had all the Winnie the Pooh characters. I think Pooh was a stoner . . . he always had the munchies. Tigger was on coke; he was always hyper and jumping around. Christopher Robin was tripping on acid; he talked to the animals, and they talked back. But Owl was deep and philosophical, and I'm guessing he was on morphine. I feel like I have entered the Matrix as I watch the doctors and nurses bustle around me. Is this real? Or is it all an illusion? Speaking of *The Matrix*, I think Keanu Reeves might have died years ago and was cryogenically frozen . . . He never ages. Wow, I'm having some super deep thoughts. I can see why Keats and Baudelaire dug the poppy train; it's like a warm blanket that wraps around you from the inside out while simultaneously making you brilliant.

"Are you feeling a little better?" the nurse asks, as she wheels a machine up to the side of my gurney.

"I feel so much better. Do I have to leave now?" I ask, sensing the party is over.

"No. Why would you have to leave? The doctor was just waiting for the medicine to subside your pain so that he can examine you and figure out what's wrong," she answers with a smile. Oh my God, I love this nurse. I love this emergency room. I need to give her a compliment or a pithy something or other to let her know how much I appreciate them giving a shit about me.

"You're really pretty. You should be a model," I say, smiling up at her.

She laughs. "That's really sweet of you, honey, but I'm five-four and pushing forty."

"No, really, I mean, look at Keanu Reeves. It's all about being cryogenically frozen." I am impressed with my insight, but she is giggling again.

"Okay, honey, the doctor will be with you shortly," she says, patting me on the shoulder and walking away.

I like that she calls me honey, like my mom always does; it makes me feel safe. For the first time since the accident I feel protected and cared for in a sterile medical setting. Why can't every doctor and nurse treat you like family, in a chicken soup way? Is it the survival of the fittest mentality? Do they just not want to get attached because you might die? And then they'll be sad and think about you forever? Or are they overworked, sleep deprived, and desensitized because they have seen it all before? Is a job that was once interesting and a labor of love now just a paycheck and a beer after work? I've got to say, from where I stay, down here on this gurney in a stoned state of bliss, trying to forget that blood is what I piss, that it is comforting and time well spent, when a doctor or nurse isn't shuffling me out the door to charge someone else rent.

This morphine is amazing, I am now a poet, or a rapper . . . rapper is better; poets don't make money. Okay, I need to come up with a rapper name . . . something as powerful as Jay-Z, Eminem, or 50 Cent. Is it like finding your porn name (which is your first pet plus the street you grew up on)? My porn name is Buttons

Paradise, but I think my rap name should be Mor (to the) Phine because that's where all these Einstein thoughts are coming from. I am sure to be signing with Def Jam any minute now. Or maybe I need a doctor, like Dr. Dre in a Death Row sort of way. Wow, that rhymed, too. Brill (to the) iant.

"Now, this is going to be a little cold," the doctor says, as he squirts a jellylike substance on my stomach and moves it around with a wand attached to the machine next to me.

"Well, from the sonogram it looks like you have a kidney stone. You're one tough cookie. It took you four days to come to the emergency room? It looks like the stone is about ready to drop into your bladder, and once that happens the pain will be gone, and in a day or two the stone will come out in your urine. Would you mind if some of my students look at this?" he asks politely.

"Sure, they can look. Could I have some more morphine, please?"

He gives me another bag of morphine (God bless his little MD heart), as six young future medicos gather around to look at my insides. "The patient's symptoms are vomiting, urinating blood, and extreme pain in the left flank. You can see here on the sonogram that the patient has a kidney stone. They say the pain is the equivalent of giving birth," the doctor lectures.

"Actually, it's like giving birth to a baby elephant through the eye of a needle," I interrupt. "But this morphine is excellent; I recommend that you give it to all your future patients. It's much better than Tylenol."

The doctor gives me a cup to pee in for the next two days, and a scheduled appointment for a follow-up with a urologist, and sends me on my way.

The emergency room nurse finds me roaming the halls of the hospital, crying and high as a kite.

"Honey? Didn't we release you an hour ago?" she asks in a soothing way.

"I can't find the exit." I weep. I feel like I need to say something to thank her for her kindness "This is my pee cup," I add, holding it up like a trophy.

⁓⁓⁓

A urologist has determined after analyzing my stone and urine that the kidney stone was probably caused by my steroid injections. According to my no-fault claims adjuster, the stone is not a direct result of the accident, so they won't cover my two-thousand-dollar emergency room and urologist visits. I don't have two thousand dollars. I don't even have two hundred dollars. I have gone through all my savings and maxed out my credit card. My recurring accident dreams have now been replaced with nightmares of living in a cardboard condo in Washington Square Park with all my belongings in a shopping cart. I don't know what to do, so I go to my lawyer's office to get advice from my go-to guy, Legal Eagle.

"Are you sure there isn't anyone you can ask for money?" he questions, with a hopeful look on his face.

I can't even speak because I'm afraid that if I open my mouth I will just start crying, so I simply shake my head.

"Well, there are companies that will loan you money against your settlement, but they charge up to a hundred percent interest. So if you borrow fifteen thousand, you might have to pay them back thirty thousand when your case settles. I don't recommend it, but if there is really no one you can ask, I'll put you in touch with them. You should also apply for food stamps and Social Security Disability."

"I can't go on food stamps. That's for poor people," I cry.

He tries to reassure me. "There is nothing to be embarrassed about; that's what food stamps are there for."

Because the truth is, I *am* poor people.

CHAPTER SEVEN

Paris Hilton, the Food Stamp Vegan

It's strange what people cling to when they lose their health, or their money, or in my case both. Some look to religion, others to drugs or liquor. I, being a fashionista, am clinging to my wardrobe, or should I say what's left of it. To the average person this might seem silly, frivolous even, but to me it makes perfect sense: if I have the right outfit on I feel like my old self, even though I am in constant pain, walking like an eighty-year-old, borrowing money from loan sharks, and about ready to apply for food stamps.

There wasn't a lot of money to be had in my formative years. Most of the time my brother, my mom, and I outfitted ourselves at secondhand stores (one person's trash is another's treasure). I started reading *Vogue* at the age of eight, scouring the pages for the latest trends that I could duplicate on a shoe-string budget. Style is not mutually exclusive to those who have money. The only thing that separates the haves from the have nots when it comes to style is imagination, and I had plenty of that. In middle school and high school, fashion was a competition, and I was competing against girls that had clothing allowances that could buy a small country, or at least buy out the designer section of a department store. I remember one year I wrote down everything I wore, refusing to duplicate the same outfit in a month . . . which sent me fishing in my brother's and mother's closets, where I discovered a plethora of fashionable finds to mix and match. My brother's ripped jeans looked adorable once I matched them with a blazer from my mom's closet and topped it off with my white T-shirt and a man's vintage tie . . . It was very boho chic. When I paired my mom's black pencil skirt with my brother's Fred Perry sweater, it magically became the perfect mod outfit. It was the hunt for the right combination of fashion fusion that excited me. Even though we were never on public assistance, my mother used to joke that we'd be the best-dressed people in the welfare line. Little did I know that one day this proclamation would come true.

I'm sure we could have qualified for food stamps or WIC (Women, Infants and Children assistance) when I was a kid, but my mother's pride would never have allowed it after the social stigma she faced when we lived, for four years, in low-income housing. Some friends stopped speaking to her, and certain children's parents wouldn't allow them to come over for play dates. She used to call our apartment the Rock, as if we were doing time in our own personal Alcatraz. As a child, I never understood why she was embarrassed of our address. But now, as I face standing on a welfare line, I feel an overwhelming sense of shame and failure, and the only thing that is keeping me sane is my new motto: One must always be appropriately dressed, even when one is applying for food stamps. I am looking at my closet full of beautiful clothes, and nothing is really screaming "food stamps." Should I wear my Helmut Lang? Or my Juicy Couture? I think it's a Juicy day . . . This cute little combo of a blue terry-cloth sweat suit says, "Juicy girls don't need food stamps. Food stamps need them." Actually, this Juicy girl does need food stamps, but she's bringing sunglasses for an incognito exit.

I received a card from my mother yesterday with the words *Don't open until Monday* written on the envelope. My mother is famous for her cards, which she sends for even the most insignificant occasion—as long as Hallmark makes a card for it, she'll send it—and I always get three cards on my birthday (two funny, and one sweet and sappy). My favorite card last year read, *Some day when I'm older, I'll smoke and drink and I'll be the biggest whore this little town has ever seen,* and on the inside she wrote, *See, dreams do come true! Happy Birthday—I gotcha! Love you, Mom!* I have a feeling this is a "Cheer up—you're on welfare!" card. I open the envelope, and the card has a very chic 1950s lady on the front and reads, *Style is like the clap, you've either got it or you haven't. And you've got it.* On the inside she's written, *I want you to go in there with your head held high. I got a little extra money last week, but the enclosed check for fifty dollars is fun money and not to be spent on anything practical. I want you to go get a manicure and pedicure, and one of your chai tea thingies, and you walk into that food stamp office feeling good. I love you Doll Face xo Mom.*

Sporting a fresh mani and pedi, and on a chai tea high, I hobble into the food stamp office feeling confident in my wardrobe selection. That is, until I notice that everyone is staring at me. I no longer have my neck and back brace Wounded Wear that lets everybody know I am injured. After wearing them for several months my muscles were starting to atrophy, and my doctor told me not to use them anymore. So now I'm just some woman in a Juicy sweat suit who walks funny. I guess I do stick out, being one of two white women in the waiting room. The other one is missing six of her front teeth and carrying on a rather heated discussion with the wall. This place looks more like a classroom than a waiting room. It has the same Band-Aid-colored floors that most classrooms have, and there are no chairs to sit in, only old school desks. I am getting an overwhelming feeling that maybe they are trying to tell us something subliminally. As I approach the woman at the front desk to take a number, I'm a little surprised that she doesn't give me a tardy slip and send me to the principal's office.

I take a seat in an uncomfortably small school desk and instantly discover that one of the legs is shorter than the others, which is causing it to rock back and forth, jarring my injured spine. I could move, but after the way I got stared at upon my entrance, I think I'll stick with the makeshift rocking chair. Speaking of sticking, why is my pants leg sticking to the bottom of the desk? I slide my hand under to investigate. There is a plenty-pack's worth of chewed-up gum under there. It seems that people have also left their mark on the top of the desk: "T + D = Love" (in a heart), "Tenisha was here," "redrum," a rather lame drawing of a penis, "Here I sit brokenhearted, tried to shit but only farted" . . . Okay, after the gum I can't take much more. Besides, that should only be written on a bathroom stall. Right? Unless they . . . okay, I can't even go there.

The waiting room is crowded. There are lots of mothers with children, and elderly people. There is even a uniformed police officer with her four kids . . . I guess fighting crime doesn't pay. How have we all gotten here? None of us probably have anything in common, except that we are living under the poverty line . . . *I* am living under the poverty line. God, that has an awful ring to it.

The two Latin women next to me are chatting and laughing. I wish I spoke Spanish 'cause I could use a good giggle right now, but the only words I know are *beer*, *bathroom*, and *money*—all immensely helpful words when on vacation in Mexico. I do, however, know Pig Latin, and itway uckssay eingbay away elfareway eenquay.

I am staring at the domestic violence poster taped to the wall as if it were a Picasso painting, trying not to look at the woman who has stopped yelling at the wall and has moved on to her own personal Donner Party, picking her nose and eating it.

A child cries. Another number is called, and I am a little jealous of the elderly man reading his book in the corner, which is the perfect way to pass the time during this grueling wait. Reading these days is frustrating for me because as soon as I finish a page I have forgotten what I just read, thanks to my short-term memory problems. I had to fight for the privilege to read as a child, due to my dyslexia. But through hard work I eventually overcame it, and reading became a pleasure instead of a torturous endeavor, and now that pleasure has been taken away from me. I watch him turn each page as the sun through the window casts shadows on his lined and etched face, and as the seconds turn into minutes, and the minutes into hours, the shadows move and change like a sundial across the architecture of his face. He smiles occasionally, as something he reads amuses him. He is in another world that the author has created, which has nothing to do with hunger or poverty, and I envy his escape.

After three hours my number is called, and I go back into the maze of cubicles to meet my caseworker, Mrs. Johnson, a middle-aged woman who looks about as warm and as fuzzy as a porcupine. She is seated behind a disheveled desk with her head cocked back, and is looking me up and down with a smirk on her face.

"Well, well, well . . . and what are you doing here, Paris Hilton?"

I want to say, I am looking for my dog, Tinkerbell, so I can shove her up your government-employee ass. Instead, I just burst into tears.

"Oh, don't cry. I was only kidding . . . I mean we don't see your type very often. So why are you here?"

I launch into a full account of what I have been through. I don't hold anything back, like I do when I talk to my brother or my friends or even my mother. I let this bitch have it . . . the truth. I tell her about the accident, my insurance woes, the hurdles I had to go through to get medical attention, the constant pain I live with, the financial ruin it has caused, and the fear that I might not make it through. I spare no detail as I describe the express train to hell that is my life. By the end of my diatribe, Mrs. Johnson has tears welling in her eyes.

"Oh, you poor girl . . . Now, normally you would have to wait for a letter of approval, but I am stamping you approved immediately. You can pick up your card tomorrow, and you take care of yourself."

I have been issued a food stamp card with a rather unattractive picture of myself on it. I will now be allotted 141 dollars a month for food, which breaks down to about four dollars and seventy-something cents a day. That's what we poor folk are allowed to eat a day . . . four dollars and seventy-something cents' worth of food. That's less than the cost of one chai tea at Starbucks. The poverty diet beats the shit out of Jenny Craig any way you cut it.

The card is in the middle of my kitchen table, just begging to be used, but I don't have the fortitude to accept it quite yet. I find myself picking it up and staring at it in disbelief several times over the past day. I am scared of this little piece of plastic, scared to walk into a grocery store and use it, scared of what it says about me. If I use this card in public, I am branding myself a failure.

There is a stigma attached to people on public assistance in this country—that they are lazy, that they should get a job, that they have a welfare mentality—and it has clearly crept into my subconscious and is wreaking havoc on what little ego I have left. We live in a society that tells kids to clean their plates because there are children starving in China. People are quick to donate money to the poor and hungry in Third World countries but look down their noses at the poor and hungry outside their own front doors. The only sign of laziness I saw in the food stamp office yesterday was from my caseworker, who initially thought it was easier to judge me than to put herself in my position and show compassion, until I shoved my story down her throat. Why should I even have to tell my story to a trained professional who is paid to aid the poor? Do these people not know what it does to the human spirit to say the three hardest words in the English language: Please help me? And yet there are so many who need that help. According to the FNS (U.S. Department of Agriculture's Food and Nutritional Service), in 2004, 84 percent of all food stamp households contained a child, an elderly person, or a disabled nonelderly person. These households received 89 percent of all food stamp benefits.

Approximately 23.9 million people in an average month in 2004 were receiving food stamps. (By 2010, this number will have jumped to approximately 44.1 million due to the recession.)

I am starting to realize that most of us walk a tightrope in this country. It just takes one illness, one more kid, one lost job, or a split-second traffic accident to shatter the delicate balance of your life, and before you know it, you are a welfare queen. And this welfare queen has one friggin' ugly picture on her food stamp card. Poverty isn't pretty at all.

It has taken me three days to work up the courage to go food stamp shopping. I can't go to the grocery store on my block because they know me there, and I would just die if they knew I was on welfare, so I am shuffling a whole nine blocks away to a grocery store where I am sure not to know anyone. I'm feeling a little anxious, my stomach is in my throat, and no matter how many times I swallow, it won't go back down where it belongs. My heart is racing, and I can feel the perspiration growing on my forehead. My back is killing me, and the pain is shooting down my right leg. I have already hugged a few garbage cans and leaned on a few buildings on my journey of defeat. In short, I am having a poverty panic attack.

Arriving at the grocery store, I stand outside for a few minutes watching floods of customers parading out with their bags full of epicurean delights, while repeating in my head what my lawyer Legal Eagle said to me: "There is nothing to be embarrassed about, that's what food stamps are there for." And after three deep breaths I am pushing my cart down the aisles slowly, picking out my food. Tofu, $2.00 . . . a bag of lentils, $1.30 . . . pasta, $2.00 . . . a bag of brown rice, $3.00 . . . natural peanut butter . . . forget it, too expensive. Hot dogs are cheaper than broccoli, potato chips are less expensive than a bell pepper, fresh orange juice is $3.90, and sugar-laden soda is $1.60. Being a vegan on food stamps is going to be a challenge . . . junk food is a lot cheaper. And we wonder why we have an obesity problem in this country. When did eating healthy become a luxury? It's as if the food industry is saying to the poor, "let them eat cake." And whoever sets the mandate of what people on food stamps are allotted to spend obviously hasn't been grocery shopping in the past twenty years because $4.70 a day doesn't get you very much, at least not much that's healthy.

I walk around a little more, just working up my nerve. Come on, Hogan; it looks like a credit card. Nobody will ever know. You just punch in your pin number and you're done.

I finally make it to the checkout line. Now, who is the worst person that I could possibly run into at this point? Yes, Miss Depressistan of the Cocktail Mafia, Sylvia Plath, just got in line behind me.

"Hogan. Oh my God. Your accident, so horrible. I zink about it all ze time. I even vrote a poem about it, called 'Vaitress Zrough a Vindshield.'"

"Oh, that's so sweet, but I'm really in a hurry."

I can only imagine how her poem must sound . . .

She used to be pretty
Now her face and body are riddled with pain
She used to be popular
Now nobody remembers her name
She used to have everything

Till the car that hit her took it all away
It would have been better had she
died that fateful day . . .

"How would you like to pay?" the cashier asks me.

I look at Sylvia and then back at the cashier. I am trapped in a Kafkaesque way. I just want to disappear—beam me up, Scotty. Now the entire Cocktail Mafia will know how truly pathetic my life has become. I will be the subject of idle gossip at the waitress station as they count their tips and sip champagne at the end of their shifts!

"Oh . . . um . . . food stamps," I say in an audible whisper.

"Slide your card and punch in your pin number," the cashier instructs.

The look on Sylvia's face says it all, and for once I agree with her; it is depressing. I'm sure she'll go home and pop a bottle of Zoloft. I, on the other hand, will go home and try to make a nutritious vegan meal for four dollars and seventy-something cents. Tofu, $2.00 . . . a bag of brown rice, $3.00 . . . reduced-sodium soy sauce, $2.50 . . . Trying to make this meager haul last two days? Priceless.

〜〜〜〜〜〜

"Hey, Gayle, it's me, Hogan. Guess who's a welfare queen? Call me back when you have a chance," I say, leaving a message on my BFF's answering machine. If anyone can get me laughing about my recent induction into the wonderful world of food stamps, it's Gayle—if she ever calls me back.

Gayle and I met sophomore year of high school. It was a perfect California day, the sun was shining, the birds were chirping, and I was dying of boredom in math class. I cracked a joke under my breath about how the teacher made math about as interesting as watching paint dry. The girl sitting to my right dressed in all black with a pierced nose laughed, and the rest is history. I think we both knew early on that we would be friends for life.

Gayle's mother suffered from severe depression and would take to the couch in her pajamas, watching TV and chain-smoking in an almost catatonic state for weeks at a time. Although Gayle knew that depression was an illness, it was hard to be the child and the caregiver, so she would escape to my house for some sense of normality. My mother has always referred to Gayle as her other daughter, and she is the closest thing I have ever had to a sister. She did, however, go MIA for most of senior year because she hated my boyfriend. But after I dumped the rat bastard we reconnected at senior prom, and we locked ourselves in the bathroom during the swanky hotel after-party, smoking cigarettes and catching up, leaving our dates to fend for themselves.

When I moved to Europe to model, Gayle and I stayed up the entire night before my flight making music mixes and chatting, wondering how we were ever going to survive the separation. Every trip back to the States was spent with Gayle and my mom. One year I had to come home to get my four impacted wisdom teeth pulled, and Gayle managed to pull a muscle in her back at the same time. So we camped out in my mom's living room for three days watching old movies, Gayle with a heating pad on her back and me with my mouth full of bloodied gauze. "Do the runway walk again," Gayle would laugh from the couch. And up I would get, with my cheeks swollen like a chipmunk, and saunter around my mother's living room in pajamas and four-inch heels, doing my best Naomi Campbell, just to make her laugh.

I had been back in New York a little over a year when I received a phone call from Gayle saying that she was breaking up with her boyfriend, dropping out of school, and that I should find us an apartment because she was moving to New York. I was beaming with excitement . . . We would be like Thelma and Louise (minus the cliff dive) or Laverne and Shirley. We would have parties, go to parties, audition, and get acting jobs together, but more important, we would have a person in this big city that we could call a true friend.

I found us a newly renovated apartment in Nolita that was about as big as a postage stamp. It had one common room that was the kitchen/dining room. Off to the right would be my tiny bedroom, and off to the left was the bathroom and what would be Gayle's tiny bedroom. The floor had a slight slope to it, the old windows rattled when it was windy, the radiator made loud banging noises when the heat came on, but it had charm in a dollhouse sort of a way. I signed the lease and waited for Gayle's arrival.

Gayle drove to New York in a Budget moving van, with all her worldly possessions and her pet snake, Emma Louise. And as she pulled up to park in front of our new apartment, she was pulled over by the police. "Ma'am, are you aware that you just sideswiped four blocks of parked cars in Little Italy?" the officer asked.

"I was wondering what all those bells were," Gayle responded.

"Those were car alarms, ma'am. You managed to take off at least ten side mirrors that we counted."

"I'm sorry. You're not going to arrest me, are you? I just drove here from North Carolina, and I really have to pee."

The officer did not arrest her, but he made her promise not to drive the moving van again. My best friend had entered New York with a bang.

The first month was great. We set up the apartment. We got her a waitressing job at the place I was working. But a month later the owner decided to clean house and fire the entire staff, all except Gayle. Gayle, however, quit in solidarity. So now we were both unemployed. Then something started happening . . . I would leave the apartment and Gayle would be lying on her bed, in her pajamas watching TV, and I would come back eight hours later and she would be in the exact same position. She was losing weight, which will happen when you only eat one muffin a day. And she didn't want to talk about it. "I'm fine," she'd say, but she wasn't fine at all. I wasn't sure what was happening to my best friend. Was it the breakup with her boyfriend? Was it the fact that she dropped out of school? Was New York just too much for her? I knew she was scared that she was slipping into the same depressive state of mental illness that her mother had battled her entire life, and I was scared, too. This went on for two months until Gayle decided to go visit her parents in California. I encouraged her to go even though I knew she would probably not be coming back. My friend was in trouble, and she had to do what she had to do.

Gayle left all her worldly possessions and her pet snake, Emma Louise. The snake and I had ignored each other up to this point, but now its livelihood was in my hands. I would have to clean its tank and feed it dead mice once a week. It didn't matter that I had ophidiophobia and was completely petrified of the python, or that I was a vegan and my PETA-loving heart wouldn't allow me to kill the mice; my friend needed me, and I would just have to man up. I struck a deal with the pet store—for an extra dollar they would make sure the mice weren't breathing, so I wouldn't have to do the dirty work myself. I would walk home with the dead mice in a brown paper bag and cautiously dump them in Emma Louise's abode. Cleaning the tank was a whole other story. I ended up letting the snake loose in my apartment while I did it, which required having one of my guy friends come over to snake-charm her back into the tank if she hissed at me or coiled herself up in one of my motorcycle boots.

Gayle eventually came back three months later, but only to pick up Emma Louise and her clothes. "Are you mad at me for bailing on you?" she asked, and of course I said no—how could I be mad at her? I was just happy that she was feeling better.

Even though Gayle couldn't live in New York, and lives with her husband in Oregon now, she loves to visit me at least once a year. And I have to say, she is the only person that I won't kill for using my toothbrush . . . She never asks, mind you, but she somehow always manages to forget hers. She was actually visiting me right before the accident. She went to the airport, and I went to work and got hit by a car.

She called a lot to check on me for the first few months after the accident, but her calls became fewer, and now they are nonexistent. I just want to laugh with my best friend about my new welfare-queen status . . . but I'm getting the sneaking suspicion that she has quit speaking to me, since this is the seventh message I have left for her over the past two months and she hasn't returned a single one. I'm not sure what I could have done to make her angry. Maybe I'm a bit depressing to talk to? I don't have news anymore about exciting parties, famous people I've recently met, or a new great play I'm acting in. My conversation is limited to what's going on in my life now, which is doctors appointments, constant pain, and food stamps.

So, in addition to my health, savings, and self-esteem, my injuries have taken my best friend as well. I thought I had three people whom I could confide in, who would have my back no matter what, but now it is apparent that I actually only have two—Mary Jane and my mom. As much as it breaks my heart to lose my best friend when I need her the most, I have bigger fish to fry right now, and maybe down the road, in a far-off tomorrow, we will lock ourselves in a bathroom like we did at senior prom, and smoke cigarettes and catch up.

Now that I have gotten food stamps out of the way, it is time to do the other thing that Legal Eagle told me to do: apply for Social Security Disability. You can't apply until you have been injured or sick and unable to work for six months. Some days it seems like the accident happened only yesterday; other days it seems like I've been dealing with this shit for years, but in reality it has been six months, and it just seems to be getting funner by the second. Legal Eagle told me that most people hire a lawyer who specializes in disability cases to help navigate the labyrinth of Social Security. Of course, they're on the take just like everyone else: the loan-shark companies that charge up to 100 percent interest; the personal injury lawyers that take one-third of your settlement; and now the Social Security Disability lawyers that take 25 percent of what you are awarded in benefits. Everybody seems to be getting ahead, while I'm just trying to survive. Screw that. I'll deal with Social Security on my own.

Appropriately dressed in a T-shirt that reads "Bu$h and $ons Incorporated. Formally Known as the U$A," I walk in to the Social Security office and manage to find a seat in between a three-hundred-pound woman with an oxygen tank and a man who keeps hitting himself in the head while he recites the alphabet. It's the only seat in the crowded waiting room, so I'm just going to have to live with the ABCs and pray that this guy doesn't get bored of his head and start hitting me.

"Hogan? Hi. I thought that was you," a woman says, approaching me. She used to teach a yoga class that I took, but I can't remember her name. Not shocking, since it's an effort to remember my own name these days. "God, this place is a zoo. I've been waiting an hour," she says, doing a visual scan of the room. I think she's trying not to stare at ABC man, but that's going to be next to impossible, even for a yogi. "I got my wallet stolen last week, and I need to get a new Social Security card."

I don't want to tell her why I am here. I don't want to talk about the accident. I don't want to talk about all my injuries, and I don't want her pity. Not that I get a chance to refuse to tell her all these things, since she doesn't even ask what I'm doing here. "Oh, that's my number," she says, looking at the digital board. "Well, it was great seeing you." She puts her hands together, bows her head slightly, and says, "Namaste" before she walks away.

I hate these government offices. I hate asking for help. I hate that I am in constant pain. I hate that I have to beg for medical care and financial assistance, and I hate the guy I suddenly hear coughing like a coal miner. I slowly look up to view the man seated in front of me hacking his lungs out, and immediately I don't feel sorry for myself anymore. Every breath is an effort for him; every inhale a labored wheeze, every exhale a meaty cough. He's a big man, with kind eyes, a pale complexion, and a T-shirt that reads "9-11-2001 Gone But Not Forgotten, NYFD." He was probably a first responder, one of the guys lucky enough to live, one of the ones who stayed at Ground Zero for months digging through the wreckage because he believed in the value of human life and the land of the free and home of the brave. And here he sits by me in the Social Security office, begging for a little help from the government of the country he helped to protect. I want to say something to him, thank him or tell him that everything will be all right, but I can't even help myself right now, and at the moment, I'm not sure that anything will ever be all right ever again for any of us seated in this waiting room.

Alphabet man is at it again, reciting his ABCs and pounding his head in a ritualistic manner, and just as my number appears on the digital board three hours after I have arrived, I realize his problem: he only goes from *A* to *W*. I might not be able to help a hero, but as I slowly get up I look at him and say, "There's three more letters . . . you forgot *X*, *Y*, and *Z*." He glances at me for a second, then looks back down again, pounds his head, and starts with *A*.

I walk back to meet my caseworker, a middle-aged man with a beard and Coke-bottle glasses, seated behind a desk. "Please sit down, Miss Gorman. I have gone over your file and your medical records, so I am just going to ask you a few questions and enter the data in my computer." He places his fingers on his keyboard and types as he speaks. "So, on March 4, 2004, you were struck by a car while crossing the street, is that correct?" I nod. "So, on March 4, 2004, you were struck by a car while crossing the street . . . Is that correct?" I nod again. "I'm sorry, Miss Gorman, you are going to have to answer me verbally; I'm blind."

I answer the rest of his questions verbally.

"Okay, Miss Gorman, you will receive a letter in the mail with your appointment to be examined by the Social Security doctors. Don't miss or cancel your appointment or you will have to wait several months to be rescheduled."

It's a month after I applied for disability, and I have finally received a letter with my appointment to see the Social Security doctor: the day after I am scheduled to have knee surgery. I can't change the surgery date, and Social Security has made it abundantly clear that I can't cancel this appointment, so I'll just have to bite the bullet. And if I ever meet that Murphy person who wrote the law "Whatever can go wrong will go wrong," I'm going to put that bullet in his head.

CHAPTER EIGHT

Crazy Juice, My Hip-Hop Knight, and Labeled "Disabled"

"Hi, honey, it's Mom. I got your message. Are you fucking crazy? Over my dead body are you having surgery without me being there."

I guess she didn't buy my I'll-be-fine-it's-only-a-little-surgery voice mail. When I was born, the doctor cut the umbilical cord, but for my mother it is like a phantom limb. She knows when I'm in pain, and she knows when I need her the most. So needless to say . . . I have no say. She will be here for my surgery because, as she says, "Mother can be a hyphenated word." So it's best not to argue with her. I don't know how she is going to financially swing coming to New York again, but knowing her, if she has to take off her belt and strap herself to the wing of the plane, she will.

─────

Anytime you go under the knife there is always the possibility that you could kick the bucket, bite the dust, cash in your chips, or, my favorite, be pushing up daisies. It's not that I am macabre, but since I shouldn't have survived the accident, according to the laws of physics and statistics, I am technically living on borrowed time, and there are things that I must attend to in case I don't make it off the table:

1. Cremation or burial? It's a tough call between "burn baby burn" and "the worms crawl in and the worms crawl out." But my Irish family will probably want to make sure I am dead, so an open casket it is . . . We micks are crepe hangers like that.

2. My brother and my mother should never have to find my rabbit vibrator, my pocket rocket, my love letters from ex-boyfriends, or my rambling journals if they have to clear out my apartment postmortem. Although those things have brought me much pleasure in life, I am quite positive that they would have an Irish wake, which would include copious amounts of grief alcohol, and one of them would think it appropriate to have these items placed with me in the aforementioned open casket, and I prefer that my family and friends remember me as the vestal virgin that I wasn't. So I will go to the bank and put them in my safety deposit box. I'm sure the Citibank employees have seen stranger deposits.

3. Cross out all people in my address book who I hate. If I didn't like them in life, I sure as hell don't want them at my funeral. This does not include any of my ex-boyfriends, however, because I am one of those people who are still friends with (almost) all their exes, and I am pretty sure I was the best

girlfriend that they have ever had, and I want them to cry long and hard for at least a day. After that, they can mourn my loss in the arms of the nearest stripper.

4. Take care of the bikini line. I don't want the mortician to think I'm an unkempt woman. After all, he will be in charge of my postmortem appearance, and if I give the wrong impression, I might be buried in a hippie dress with unflattering makeup.

5. I should have a will, but I have no worldly possessions worth speaking of besides my wardrobe, and I would like to be buried with it like the Egyptian pharaohs, because the after-party is sure to be better than this.

6. I should also have a living will, but I don't. So while I am still living, I will strike a deal with my mother (because I don't want any Terri Schiavo action). I'll promise to take her out in the wilderness and shoot her in the head should she ever get Alzheimer's. And if I slip into a vegetative state she can pull the plug; OD me on my new favorite, morphine; or call Kevorkian. Suffocation with a pillow is not an option due to claustrophobia.

7. Being a little type A, I need to set some guidelines for my funeral-slash-wake. I would like each mourner to get a gift bag, because when you think about it, it is my final party. The bags should read *RIP the best-dressed bitch I've ever known*. They will contain a bottle of red wine, a DVD of *Breakfast at Tiffany's*, and a gift card from Starbucks for a chai tea. I think these items are a true representation of my soul, and

they will be immensely useful to my mourners during their time of grief. Better throw in some Kleenex, too.

HOGAN'S SCHIZOPHRENIC FUNERAL SONG LIST

"It's All Over Now, Baby Blue" by Bob Dylan
"Hallelujah" by Leonard Cohen
"Parting of the Sensory" by Modest Mouse
"Another One Bites the Dust" by Queen
"Cold as Ice" by Foreigner
"Highway to Hell" by AC/DC

For my eulogy, there will be no weepy sentimental BS. In fact, nobody I know is allowed to speak because they will all turn into crybabies, and I will have none of that. I would like my eulogy performed by special guest Fran Lebowitz. She can start out with some of her quotes, like "There is no such thing as inner peace. There is only nervousness and death." Or "All God's children are not beautiful. Most of God's children are, in fact, barely presentable." Or "I do not believe in God. I believe in cashmere." Since I do not know Miss Lebowitz and have no money to leave to pay for a speaker, I need to contact all my hot female model friends and have them show up at her home and beg her to speak, and it would be preferable if they were impeccably dressed when they did my bidding. Oh, and bearing gifts of nicotine.

Speaking of which, I would like smoking allowed at my funeral, along with passed hors d'oeuvres and an open bar. Grief calls for vices . . . That being said, my mother should be heavily sedated. (I think three valiums, a muscle relaxer, and a joint, repeated every hour, is probably in order.) And finally, as my casket is being lowered six feet under, I would like the Jam's "Going Underground" to be playing.

Now that I have planned my fantasy funeral and taken care of loose ends and any incriminating evidence, I am ready to face the knife . . . after I select pictures, approved by me, of me, for the obit. The last impression is, after all, just as important as the first impression.

My mother and I are sitting at my kitchen table having dinner, or as I am calling it, "the last supper." In twelve hours I will be in the operating room.

"Are you nervous about the surgery tomorrow?" my mom asks, taking a bite of her Portobello burger.

"A little, but it'll be fine. They'll knock me out and I'll wake up and it will all be over."

My mother is now giggling, which seems inappropriate considering the subject matter.

"What are you laughing at?"

"I'm just remembering your only other surgery. Remember Doctor D?"

"How could I forget? I had such a crush on him."

Now she is laughing so hard that there are tears rolling down her face. Has she lost her mind?

"What the hell is so funny?"

"You were a nightmare on those drugs. Sue, the recovery room nurse, told me that you were yelling at the top of your lungs that you wanted to have sex with Doctor D, and that you kept pulling up your hospital gown to show him that you didn't have underwear on, and shouting that you were ready whenever he was."

"I did what? You never told me that. All you said was that Sue said I had a foul mouth in the recovery room."

"Well, you were only thirteen."

"Exactly, I was only thirteen. I had never had sex before. I had never even kissed a guy, and I was talking like that? Can you imagine what I could possibly say now?" I exclaim in horror.

"Oh, I can imagine. You better pray they have a muzzle in the recovery room or that your cute doctor is out of earshot."

This information is not helping quell my fears of being cut open tomorrow; in fact, my anxiety level is a ten on the Richter scale.

"I thought they couldn't reveal what is said due to doctor-patient confidentiality, or that Hippocratic oath thing?" I ask, hoping that she is kidding.

"Well, they're not supposed to, but I worked at the hospital, and they do talk about the crazy things people say postsurgery; they just don't tell the patient."

Holy shit . . . I was worried about the possibility of dying in surgery, but this is far more worrisome. Obviously, being drugged-out is like sexual truth serum for me.

I am starving, uncaffeinated, and I look like a tool in my hospital gown and surgical cap. You'd think some designer would have updated hospital garb to something a little more flattering that doesn't involve your butt hanging out. I think I've already managed to moon a couple of nurses just walking from the bathroom to the presurgery room.

I am lying on a gurney, trying to think of happy things that have nothing to do with being cut open, blood, or death. This is proving to be harder than expected with the nurse who keeps interrupting me to ask which knee I am having surgery on, and it is a little worrisome that I've answered "the right knee" three times and she just asked me again. I thought I was the one with the brain injury? Thankfully, she won't be the person cutting me open, because I would probably wake up missing my appendix.

Speaking of cutting open, Dr. McBones has just arrived, dressed in a Nike tracksuit with a messenger bag across his shoulders. He must have come from the gym, where he was working on his perfect body. God, he looks dreamy. And suddenly, I'm not nervous anymore. His sexy presence is like an instant hit of Xanax.

"Hi, Hogan. How are you feeling?" he asks, as he looks down at me on the gurney with a little smile on his face.

"I'm great!" I say, a bit too energetically for this early hour. I am such a pathetic dork. *I'm great? Couldn't you think of something more appropriate for the situation?*

"Good. Now which knee are you having surgery on today?" he asks.

"The right knee," I answer.

"Which knee?" he asks again.

Oh my God, I am at Hospital Crazytown, where everybody has lost their minds. This is a horror movie, and I am about ready to be the next victim.

"The right. Why does everybody keep asking that?" I question, fearing for my life.

"We have to for legal reasons," he answers with a chuckle, taking a Sharpie out of his messenger bag and making an *X* on my right knee, like a treasure map.

"Well, FYI, it's a little repetitive. I thought you all were suddenly stricken with amnesia or that my short-term memory loss was contagious." He is chuckling again. Score one for the gimp.

"Okay, well, I'm going to get changed, and I'll see you in a few minutes," he says, patting me on the shoulder before he walks away.

I love when a man tells me he's going to get changed and he'll see me in a few minutes. That's sexy. Okay, someone needs to focus. I am having surgery, not going on a date. Actually, I can't even think Dr. McBones is hot right now. I must eradicate all sexual feelings that I have for him because otherwise I might yell that I want to have sex with him, show him my vajayjay, and tell him that I'm ready whenever he is; and that would be bad . . . very, very, bad.

As they wheel me into the operating room I see Dr. McBones waiting. God he even looks hot in scrubs. Stop . . . bad thought . . . he is ugly. Just imagine he is Carrot Top. There is also a stereo in the corner. If they put something foul on, like Coldplay, when they are filleting my knee, I could possibly flatline on the table.

"Do you play music in surgery?" I ask.

"Sometimes."

"Well, I'd like to be the DJ, and I'm thinking Dylan." After all, "Blood on the Tracks" would be very appropriate.

"Okay then. Now, I can hear in your voice that you have a slight cold, so we are not going to put you completely under. We're going to give you something that will make you not remember the surgery, though."

Oh no . . . this is bad. "Will I be able to talk?"

"Yes . . . so if you can feel anything, you'll be able to tell us,"

Dr. McBones says just as the anesthesiologist gives me the crazy juice.

I need to give him a disclaimer, or something, to warn him that I might turn into Jenna Jameson. "Well, if I say anything stupid . . ." And then I'm out . . . or so I think.

———

I am slowly coming to in the recovery room, and as my eyes regain focus, I see Dr. McBones standing over my bed, smiling in his cute little way. He's smiling . . . Does that mean I kept my mouth shut? Or did I offer to sexually service him?

"Did you have a nice rest?" he asks, looking down at me. I nod.

"There was a lot more damage than the MRI showed. Not only were your meniscus and ACL torn, but there was a chunk off the back of your kneecap just floating around. So I repaired the torn ligaments and removed the loose matter." Forget that . . . I want to know if I was bragging about my hand job ability in surgery. "You are not, under any circumstances, to get your leg wet or remove the bandages. I'll see you in my office in a week." Okay, phew. I guess I kept things G-rated.

———

My mother managed to get me home from the hospital as I was doing my best Courtney Love impression, sprawled out across the back seat of the cab. I vaguely remember insisting that we stop at Starbucks to get a chai tea because "I didn't get a fucking lollipop."

It's three hours later, and the anesthesia is doing a backflip in my stomach, and the pain is unbearable. I have turned into

Pukeahontas, and let's just say it's a little hard to lean over the toilet with your knee bandaged up. I have just finished my second tour of duty in the bathroom and am sitting at the kitchen table with my leg stretched out in front of me wondering if the torment will ever stop.

"Well, the bathroom's all clean," my mother says in her best Florence Nightingale voice. "I'm just going to turn on the TV to get your mind off the pain."

And with that, my mother trips over my freshly operated-on leg.

"Oh, honey, oh, honey, I am so sorry."

The tears of agony are rolling down my face. I can't even speak, it hurts so bad. Don't yell, Hogan. This woman just flew halfway across the country to take care of you. I grit my teeth and manage to eke out, "Just . . . walk . . . away."

The surgery was yesterday, and today is my Social Security doctor's appointment, where they will determine if I am eligible for Social Security Disability benefits. With my throbbing knee bandaged up to the size of a basketball and my back spasming out of control from limping on my cane, my mother is going to have to dress me for my doctor's appointment.

"This reminds me of when you were a little girl and I used to dress you for school. You were just the cutest thing," she says, as she unfolds a T-shirt.

"That's nice but—"

"No matter how old you are, you're still my little Hogan. Now reach for the sky so I can put your shirt on . . ."

"I swear to God, if you do the rabbit through the hole when you're tying my shoes, I'll cane you."

The sight of me in the mirror is more horrifying than I could have ever imagined. It's a rather eclectic outfit of a Mickey Mouse T-shirt, a long plaid skirt, tube socks, hiking boots, and a rhinestone butterfly barrette in my hair.

"I look retarded!" I bellow.

"No you don't. You have to keep that leg covered, and you can't get pants over your bandages, and that's the only long skirt you have. You could wear one of your evening gowns, but I think you might be a little overdressed."

"I hate you."

"You better be nice to me or I'll take a picture of you before we leave."

By the time we arrive at the Social Security Disability office, I am in so much pain that I am ready to swallow a service revolver. I start to take a seat next to a young guy in a hoodie whose pants are so baggy and low that a good part of his boxer shorts are showing. Getting into the chair is harder than ever since my throbbing, injured leg must remain completely straight. I have a death grip on my cane and have to anchor myself on the back of the chair with my left hand, slowly navigating my descent down with all of the grace of a beached whale. Although swearing would be preferable, grunting is helping. I am, after all, a lady, and I don't think my fellow injured Americans really need their already stressful wait marred by a blonde in a Mickey Mouse T-shirt screeching, "Motherfuckershitass!" The guy with the hoodie is watching me out of the corner of his eye from his slouched, arms crossed, I'm-too-cool-for-school position in the chair.

"You hurt real bad . . . don't ya?" he asks.

"Yeah."

He makes a "tss" sound like suburban teenage girls do when they are over something, shakes his head, and without looking at me says, "Man . . . I know what that's like." He pauses for a moment and then stands, as he pulls his jeans up a little so they are now only showing three inches of his underwear and strikes an intimidating stance in front of my mother. "Hey, lady, give me your coat," he orders with his hand reached out. A look of horror mixed with confusion crosses her face. He makes the "tss" sound again and shakes his head. "Don't worry, I'm not gonna steal it. I just wanna try and help your daughter."

He takes my mother's coat and folds it in a meticulous fashion, then places it on an empty chair that he's brought over. Then he gently picks up my injured leg and places it on top.

He sits back down and looks at me out of the corner of his eye, with his head slightly cocked and a proud smile on his face. "Dat makes it feel a little better . . . don't it?"

"Yeah, it does. Thank you."

My mother excuses herself to go downstairs and get some air. I think the reality that I am on welfare and now applying for disability has finally hit her. I, on the other hand, have decided to take my mind off my knee and get to know the nice guy next to me. His name is Darnell, and he was shot five times. He was working the streets at the time. I don't want to press him to find out what "working the streets" actually means, but I'm guessing he wasn't driving an ice cream truck, being that his mother had the doctors leave one of the bullets in his stomach, as a "reminder" never to be so stupid again. I am thoroughly impressed. I mean, I've never met anyone who's been shot before.

"Do ya wanna see it?" he asks, like an eight-year-old with a prized baseball card.

"Hell yeah, I want to see it," I respond with curious glee. He slowly raises his hoodie up, modestly exposing the right side of his stomach, and sure enough, there is a bullet under his skin. The scar tissue is a whitish red, contrasting his ebony complexion. This is the best show-and-tell ever.

"Your mom sounds like one tough lady."

"Yeah, she's a strong woman. I was in the hospital for six months, and she was there every morning before work and every night when she got done. And when the doctors told her I probably wouldn't walk again, she said, 'Well, then, you don't know my son very well, because Darnell is gonna walk out the door of this hospital, and you best be makin' that happen.'"

"I bet she doesn't let you out of her sight now."

"You got dat right. She told me if she ever caught me on the streets again, she'd shoot me herself."

My own mother reappears with a handful of drinks. She's gone on a Starbucks run. She even brought one for Darnell. I don't want to tell her that it probably isn't the best idea to bring in fancy drinks when you're begging the government for money because you can't work, or that each tea costs more than my food stamp allotment each day. Might as well just appreciate the gesture.

Darnell seems taken with this random act of gratitude, and I am surely taken with his random act of kindness. "Be careful, it's addicting . . . this stuff is like crack," I warn my new friend as I take a sip.

He cocks his head back, gives his signature "tss," and then laughs. "I don't know about dat . . . but it's good . . . real good."

We sit there in the waiting room savoring our chai, both quietly acknowledging that we might not be much, but our mothers love us, and solely supported by their strength, we will recover from anything.

They finally call my name, and I am escorted to X-ray. I have already been so radiated that I am sure to be glowing like Chernobyl any day now. The technician informs me that I will have to get undressed and put on a little paper robe. She has, however, taken pity on me and is letting me leave on my tube socks and hiking boots.

After ten minutes of the sorriest striptease in history, I am finally in the little paper robe that barely covers my butt.

Note to self: Wearing a G-string today was a very bad idea.

Getting up on the table is like climbing Mount Kilimanjaro, even with the technician's help, and has me so exhausted that I take a little catnap during the x-rays. I'm a pro at this by now, and can hold my breath and nod off simultaneously. The descent, however, is giving me a lovely cocktail of vertigo mixed with jaw-clenching pain.

"Okay, I'll take you to the examining room after you've changed," the technician says with a smile, massaging her left shoulder, which I might have dislocated as she helped me off the table.

"Well, is the doctor going to make me strip again? Because if he is, I'd rather save myself the humiliation and horrible pain and just stay in this Pam Anderson version of a robe."

"Yes, you're right. No need to put you through that again," she says, opening the door.

I hobble out behind her in my mini paper robe, tube socks, and hiking boots, leaning on my cane. Everybody in the waiting room is looking at me as if they are witnessing an out-of-season Halloween parade. There is utter silence. I slowly raise my head, put my nose in the air, and give my best "Blue Steel" à la *Zoolander*.

"Don't copy my style, Darnell. I know you want to."

Darnell shakes his head and laughs. "Girl, that's some crazy gear you got on."

And with that I gimp down the hallway to the examining room. The doctor is a tiny Indian man, seated behind a tiny desk, in his tiny examining room.

"Tell me about your injuries, Miss Gorman."

"Well, I was hit by a car while—"

"I did not ask you how it happened, did I?" he says, slapping his open hand down on his metal desk to emphasize his point.

"Sorry . . . I have two herniated discs in my neck and three in my lower back that cause me constant pain. I have numbness in my arms and legs. I just had surgery on my right knee yesterday to repair two torn ligaments, and I have a head injury, which—"

"Your head is not my concern," he says, slapping the desk again. "Now lie on the table so I can examine you."

"I'm not sure I can get up there. Could you help me?"

"You are very aggressive, Miss Gorman. I am not here to help you. I am here to examine you, and if you will not lie on the table, then I am done," he says with another slap. This guy must have been Mussolini in a past life.

With much moaning and pain, I manage to get on the table myself, where the doctor proceeds to move my neck and arms with complete disregard for the injuries I've just outlined for him.

"Take off the bandage on your knee, so that I can examine it."

"I can't take it off . . . I only had surgery yesterday."

"I need you to take off the bandage," he orders.

"But I can't take it off until I see my doctor next week," I plead.

"You are very aggressive—I am done then!" he shouts, raising his hands with the universal "I give up" symbol.

"Can I at least change back into my clothes in here?"

"You can change somewhere else. I have work to do."

I limp out of his office in my short paper robe and hiking boots, crying. I am quite sure his report will read "Aggressive. Aggressive. Aggressive," and that he will make it his mission in life to see that I am not approved for disability benefits.

My mother spots my tears immediately and runs to comfort me.

I was hoping to say good-bye to my hip-hop knight Darnell, but he is in an examining room. I pray his doctor is nicer than mine.

* * *

It's been three days since the surgery. Three days of gut-wrenching, unrelenting agony. The throbbing in my knee is constant, and the slightest pressure on my right leg causes a chain reaction in my body that feels like someone is hitting my knee with a sledgehammer while simultaneously punching me in the lower back. Besides the unpleasant trip to the Social Security doctor, my mother and I have been cooped up in my tiny one-bedroom apartment, and we are getting on each other's nerves. Actually, I'm getting on her nerves, and I'm getting on my own nerves. I woke up on the bitter-bitch side of the bed this morning, and someone obviously pissed in my Wheaties. Like Howard Beale says in one of my favorite movies, *Network*, "I'm mad as hell, and I'm not going to take this anymore." I am sick of feeling like a little metal ball in this pinball machine called life.

"Put on your coat. Let's get some air. I'm going to go postal if I don't get the hell out of here," I bark at my mom.

"Okay."

Luckily, I live on the first floor of my apartment building, so it's only eight small steps down to the sidewalk. Scratch that, it is eight excruciating steps, and I have a swear word for each one . . .

"Motherfucker."

"Son of a bitch."

"Dicktard."

"Asswipe."

"Cocksucker."

"Fucking fuck."

"Goddamit."

"Bitchassmotherfucker."

"Are you okay, sweetheart?" she asks once I have descended the final step.

"Yeah, never fucking better."

The sun on my face feels refreshing as we lean against my building. I am content with my huge eight achievements for a moment, until I spot a perfect blonde in peak physical condition jogging by us in her Adidas tracksuit, and suddenly I can feel the tears welling in my eyes. That used to be me, and now I'm someone who is impressed with herself for getting down eight stairs. Screw that. I need a Rocky-style training montage to lift me out of my funk and pump up my adrenaline. I'm already singing "Eye of the Tiger" (by the band appropriately named Survivor) as I limp slowly and furiously down the street, cane in hand. The pain has me ready to bite off bat heads Ozzy Osborne–style.

"Hogan . . . honey, I don't think you should be . . ." my mother ekes out with worry, trailing behind me.

"Today I am going to walk a block . . . and tomorrow I'm going to walk two blocks . . . and maybe someday, if I keep doing this and trying, I'll get my life back. So just come with me."

"Okay . . . just don't overdo it."

My mom understands persistence more than anyone. When she was little, she got polio. It was the tail end of the epidemic, and the doctors told her parents that she was lucky to be alive but that she would only walk with leg braces on for the rest of her life. Her father was a former football star at Notre Dame, and nobody was putting his baby in leg braces. So he would take her to the local swimming pool every day and train her. It was hard, but little by little, she got her legs back. And today, nobody would ever know that she almost wore leg braces for life. I come from strong stock.

Fuck it; I'm going for two blocks today.

It feels like someone is hacking my knee with an ice pick as I limp on my cane. I am doing my best impersonation of the Little Engine That Could—I think I can, indeed. The perspiration is staining the underarms of my T-shirt, and the metallic taste of pain is filling my mouth. I'm feeling lightheaded when I hit the two-block mark.

"Sweetheart, are you okay?" she asks upon hearing me hyperventilate.

"I think I might throw up."

"Well, why don't I get us a cab home?"

"It's two blocks. I'm not taking a cab." I'm a little embarrassed that I didn't factor in that if I limped two blocks, I would still have to limp back. Way to go, genius, even a six-year-old could have figured out that equation.

By the time I make it to my front door I am praying for amputation, but I'll settle for a good stiff victory drink. It's got to be seven o'clock somewhere in the world because this mama needs some medicine.

Finally, it is time for my follow-up visit with Dr. McBones.

"We've been expecting you. I heard your surgery went well," the receptionist says with a smirk.

As my mother and I walk to the examining room, all the nurses keep looking at us and chuckling.

"Since we walked in the office, nobody can look at you without laughing. You must have been a little slut in surgery. Especially with that cute doctor of yours," my mother loudly whispers. She is taking great pleasure in watching me squirm. Dr. McBones enters the examining room and is as hard to read as ever.

"Well, let's undress your knee and see how it's healing." Did he just say "undress"? Oh, Jesus. Did I ask him to undress me in surgery?

He slowly takes off the bandages. My knee is bruised and swollen, but I am overjoyed that the scars are minute and I will be back in short skirts in no time.

"Looks like it's healing nicely. Now let me show you on this model what I did," he says, handing me a plastic model of a half leg with a knee and pointing out the different parts he repaired in surgery.

"Now, here you can see the meniscus, and here . . . ah . . . Hogan, can I have my knee back?"

My nerves are causing me to shake the model knee that I am holding, and it looks like I am giving it a hand job.

"Oh . . . sorry," I say, handing the knee back to him. I am completely mortified, but on a high note, at least I know my hand is working again.

"Okay," he says, clearing his throat nervously. "Now we need to get you back into physical therapy as soon as possible and start strengthening your knee, and I want you to continue using your cane." He stands to make his exit.

"Thank you, doctor."

"You're welcome, whore."

No, I'm kidding, he didn't really say that, but it would have been funny if he did. I'm sure I was horrible in surgery, but I will never know what I said thanks to that Hippocratic oath thing, which will keep this hypocrite in the dark.

As my mom and I walk out of the office, she turns to me and asks, "Sweetheart, did you notice his wedding ring?"

"No, he doesn't wear a wedding ring."

"Well, he was today."

I have been tackling my recovery like I'm training for the Special Olympics, and my present record is a ten-block limp. It involves a few rests and icing my knee afterward, but I think that's pretty good for a week and a half after surgery. My mom left today. She offered to stay until I am completely back on my feet, but she has already missed two weeks of work, and I couldn't put her behind the financial eight ball any more than she undoubtedly already is.

I have decided that my first solo mission will be the grocery store. It's good to have goals, and my cane is looking a little better with the sticker I put on it that says, "Fashion Don't." Speaking of fashion don'ts, I am very happy to be rid of the huge postsurgery bandages and be back in pants. I've got on my skinny jeans and a white T-shirt that is distressed to perfection.

I am hobbling down the block trying not to focus on the pain by thinking of things that I am grateful for: I am grateful that I am alive. I am grateful that I have an awesome mom. I am grateful that it's not butt-ass cold out, like it was last week. I am grateful for swear words, because when one is in pain they can be used as an adjective, a verb, and a noun, sometimes all in the same sentence. I am grateful that after years of modeling I have learned not to faint from hunger, because with my food stamp budget I am perpetually famished. I am grateful that I am a blonde and people just assume I am stupid, so I don't have to explain the short-term memory loss. I am grateful for the person that just decided to water their plants on their fire escape right as I'm walking under it.

This grateful stuff is proving to be harder than I thought. "Hey, you might want to look down before you water your illegal foliage."

"Well, maybe you should walk faster," the mystery horticulturist bellows.

"Well, maybe you should come down here so I can shove my cane up your ass."

I hate people right now, especially one particular woman with a green thumb. I look like a contestant in a wet T-shirt contest, thanks to her. I should probably go home and change, but getting up and down my stairs is almost as big of a bitch as she is. Retreating is not an option. I am soldiering on, transparent T-shirt and all.

I have just turned the corner to begin block two. Every Saturday there is a punk concert on this block, with hordes of people in their best Sid Vicious gear, hanging out on the street to get into the venue. I have almost made it past the Mohawks and combat boots when a guy with purple hair says, "Man, that is so cool . . . it's not that often that you see a hot cripple."

I can't believe he just called me a cripple. You can't do that. That is so un-PC that it's almost to XYZ. It's wrong and bigoted and prejudiced. Only I can call myself a cripple, and I do it in a self-deprecating way, but you can't. I don't see you limping on a cane or in braces. *You* are not part of the group. If you were injured or disabled, you would be allowed to call me a cripple, and I would say, "What's up, gimp?" But you're not, so, stranger, step softly when you walk, and don't fucking talk.

I so want to go all Rosa Parks on his wannabe punk-rock ass and blurt out this monologue in my head, but Gandhi was probably right, "An eye for an eye makes the whole world blind." Instead, I suppress the urge to berate him, or beat him with my cane, and take a cue from my Social Security hip-hop knight, Darnell: I cock my head back with a smirk, look him up and down, make the "tss" sound, and angrily limp on.

On my way back home, balancing my groceries while leaning on my cane, I hobble past a basketball court.

"Hey . . . hey," a man shouts. Of course he couldn't possibly be talking to me, so I continue limping.

"Hey, you with the cane," he shouts again.

Well, I guess he is talking to me. I slowly pivot around and look at him in all of his middle-aged, slightly sweaty, basketball-holding glory.

"Is that for reals, or are you just pretending?" he questions, point-ing at my cane.

"No, unfortunately it's real," I respond.

"Well, I'm a married man, but I gotta say you wear it well."

Is that supposed to be a backhanded compliment? It's not like it's a fashion accessory.

What is it with these guys? Do they just figure that if you're injured they can say anything they want to you, like they're throw-ing you a bone, and you should be grateful? I can't be Gandhi anymore.

"Is your fat beer gut for real, or are you just pregnant? Is your comb-over for real, or are you just going for the Donald Trump look? Oh, no, that's right, you're just married."

That's it. I am throwing out this damn cane when I get home. Either that or I'm impaling myself on it.

Someone at Social Security must have had a heart and a brain, because two months after my initial exam with the horrible In-dian doctor, I get reexamined by two other doctors. Per proce-dure, I could not apply for disability until after I could prove I was unable to work for six months. It took another month until my aggressive doctor's appointment, and then another two months until my reexamination, and then another month to get the letter . . . ten months in total for the government to decide that I am disabled. Which from what I understand is fast, and rare with-out a lawyer to handle all the bureaucracy for you—at the bargain price of 25 percent of what you are awarded.

But today I received the letter in the mail stating that I am labeled "disabled" and have been approved for Social Security Disability benefits. I'm not sure how they expect an injured person to live in New York on $747 a month when you can't even rent a room at a crack den for that. But, as my mom says, it's better than a kick in the face with a wet boot.

CHAPTER NINE

There Is No Fault; I'm Just the Public Assistance Crier

It seems that my no-fault coverage has been cut off, but they neglected to tell me. Apparently they have determined that I am not getting any better. I found out when I received a bill from my physical therapist last week with a lovely note threatening to turn it over to a collection agency if I don't pay.

The no-fault doctor who examines me every month warned me that this could happen, during my last exam. He said that it happens all the time; he writes down how injured someone is, visit after visit, and then some claims adjuster at No-Fault reviews the file and sees all the money they are paying out and that the person isn't getting any better, and then they cut them off. He probably shouldn't have told me that, since he is technically working for them. I thought at the time that he was trying to scare me, but he was really trying to warn me.

My doctors will continue to see me on a lien, which means that they will get paid when my court case settles. I'm not sure what will happen if the case doesn't go in my favor. I'm guessing that will be my financial problem. But there will be no more MRIs or tests to see if my brain and body are healing. No more procedures or surgery, so that means neck and back surgery aren't even an option for me anymore. No more physical therapy, which is the only thing that helps give me any mobility at all, and no more prescriptions, since they cost three hundred dollars a month. I don't know what I will do without the pain medication, the muscle relaxers, the anti-inflammatories, and the pills that are supposed to take down the swelling of my brain. I am in pain every second of the day even with the medications to take the edge off, and without them it will be unbearable. And if the swelling in my brain doesn't go down, will I ever get my memory back?

It's getting increasingly harder to stay positive, especially with this recent blow. I can't help but think about the man or woman seated behind a desk at No-Fault, who has never been to medical school, determining that I don't deserve to be covered anymore. I am just a faceless file to them, a number that needs to be crunched, something that must be eradicated to make their bottom line work out. I am nothing. I am no one, except a file stamped "Denied."

I feel like an alien in my own country. Every time I turn a corner I seem to hit another brick wall. My body feels like a prison. The pain is still unrelenting. Maybe they're right; maybe I'm not getting better, but I try. I never miss a doctor's appointment; I follow their instructions and take my prescriptions; I go to physical therapy (or as I like to call it, gimp gym) as if it were a religion; I eat a healthy vegan diet on a food stamp budget of four dollars and seventy cents a day; I do children's memory games on my computer to try to regain my short-term memory and strengthen my brain. I think it might be better to be an animal;

if an animal is sick or injured and not getting "any better" they are put down, so they don't have to suffer. We have a Humane Society for our four-legged friends, yet I am struggling to see any sense of humanity in the society that I am living in.

~~~~~~

It's been a month since No-Fault cut me off, and without physical therapy, my body is in a downward spiral toward hell. I do all the stretching and strengthening exercises that I can remember, but several I can't even attempt because they require equipment or assistance. I am rationing what little medication I have left by cutting each pill in half, but despite this judicious approach, my pharmaceuticals will be gone by next week. The stabbing pains in my head are back to a level ten, and my spinal column has me hunched over like Quasimodo. I still go to see all my doctors regularly, but without coverage, they can't really do anything for me, or to me, because there is no money to cover any procedures or tests.

I have, however, found a way to combat the depression: Oprah. She's better than Prozac, and the people she has on make what I'm going through look like a trip to Disneyland. I mean, my husband didn't try to kill me, I'm not a child sold into the sex trade, I'm not a seventeen-year-old meth addict, and I wasn't abducted by a pedophile. And then there are the celebs, and they might be famous now, but they haven't always had it easy. Oprah treats all her guests the same. She laughs with them, she cries with them. She's like a mother, sister, teacher, and therapist, all rolled up into one amazing O. When Oprah is talking to someone on her show and she's giving them tough love or encouragement, I feel like she's talking to me. Sometimes I nod at the TV or say, "You're right, Oprah, I am doing that," or, "Thanks, Oprah, I needed to hear that." We usually laugh at the same time or cry at the same time, and we both do the same thing where we try not to cry but we can't help it because what we are hearing from the guest is so moving, and then it turns into this ugly-cry situation where neither one of us looks attractive, and I just have to thank God that she's on TV and not me. So she's kind of taking one for our home team. She even has her own Post-it on my wall, interspersed between reminders for doctors' appointments and "Don't forget your keys," that says, "Turn on TV at 4 p.m. for your therapist Oprah." I guess you could say she's the poor man's therapist because she helps and gives advice for free.

Oprah has had some fucked-up shit happen to her. But did she let that get her down? Hell no. To adversity, she said, "Bite me." To racism, she said, "Bite me." To sexual abuse, she said, "Bite me" (maybe she didn't say "Bite me" on that last one, but you get the picture). And look at her now: she didn't climb up on a pity pot; she took the world by the balls and used that power to help people. She is always saying, "You are responsible for your own life," and I think she is right. No matter what life throws at you, you have the power to turn it around, and while I am working on turning it around, Oprah is saving my life . . . at least until four p.m. tomorrow. As Whitney Houston says, "Crack is wack," so I don't do that, but I do an hour of O power, and she's better than crack . . . she's my Prozac.

FYI, Oprah's best friend is named Gayle, too . . . Only, as far as I know, Gayle is talking to her.

~~~~~~~

Mary Jane and Bud know everything that's going on with me, and they also know that I will never ask for help. So they've gotten crafty and have asked me to babysit a few times and then grossly overpaid me. Today is one of those days, but I have to say it's not really babysitting because Peaches and Candy are two of my favorite people to hang out with, and I have better conversations with them than I do with most adults.

"Girls, remember to treat Hogan like a China doll. Don't jump on her, ask her to lift you onto the monkey bars, or make her chase you," Mary Jane instructs as she walks out the door.

"God, you make me sound like an invalid." I laugh, while simultaneously flipping her off. "Okay, ladies, now that we finally got rid of your mother, I think you should get dressed so we can go to the park."

"But Hogan, we are dressed," Candy retorts, like the smartypants that she is, wearing jeans that she grew out of about a year ago and her school uniform shirt (which should never be worn on a Saturday). Peaches, on the other hand, has on what looks to have once been a white skirt (I swear you could sit this kid in a corner and just watch the dirt grow out of her pores) and a T-shirt that says "Daddy's Girl," which she must have used to clean off her paintbrushes when she got her art on.

"No, your mother dressed you, and although she was a fabulous model, she's never had much of an eye for fashion. I want you to dress yourselves; the crazier the better. Fly your fashionista flag."

"Can I dress as a princess and really go outside?" Peaches asks.

"I don't know . . . Can you dress as a princess and go outside? As long as you're confident, you can wear anything you want, as far as I'm concerned."

"This is awesome. I don't know if I should dress as a doctor, a ballerina, or an Indian," Candy exclaims, as she tears into the bedroom.

After forty-five minutes, they finally emerge. Peaches is clad in a princess dress and tiara, with black-and-white Pippi Longstocking tights and combat boots, and is wielding a broken fairy wand. Candy is wearing a pink tutu, green tights, purple Converse high-tops, a doctor's coat with a stethoscope around her neck, and an Indian headband with a red feather, and is carrying a doll that looks like a cross between Wednesday from the Addams Family and the lead singer of the Cure. They look pretty fabulous . . . although, Candy might be showing signs of schizophrenia.

"Oh, they look so cute. Are you going to a party?" a random woman asks as we walk down the street.

"No, it was free-dress day at the children's mental hospital."

"She's kidding. We dressed ourselves, Hogan let us," Candy offers. The woman's shocked look softens into a nervous laugh before she walks away shaking her head.

"Hogan, look at that guy. He must be really tired. He's falling asleep standing up," Peaches observes. We pause for a moment to marvel at his talent. Just as he is about to fall over, he somehow manages to regain semiconsciousness and right himself up before instantly nodding off again.

"Maybe we should wake him up?" Candy questions.

"He's not asleep. He's on heroin, and unless you want to be a walking zombie, you should probably never try it." I figure this is as good a time as any for a "Just Say No" drug lecture.

"I don't want to be a zombie," Candy exclaims with her tongue out. Mission accomplished; I am officially the Nancy Reagan of the East Village.

We head to the playground, where I get out of harm's way and sit on a park bench in between the overprotective mothers of New York.

"Sammy, be careful. That ladder is too high for you," the woman next to me shouts to her rather unattractive offspring. Not to be judgy, but the poor kid looked like an anteater.

"Tarin, don't get too close to the kids swinging," another hollers.

"Sweetheart, you can't go down the slide until I can catch you, so play in the sandbox until Mommy is off the phone," a third bellows.

I feel a little left out. Luckily, Candy just hauled off and punched Peaches for cutting in front of her on the line for the swings. "Candy, stop hitting your sister. You might need a kidney someday."

The other members of the Breeders Club all turn to look at me in admonishment.

"Hogan, why would I need a kidney from Peaches?" Candy questions while running toward me, with her younger sister trailing behind. Uh-oh, now I have to actually explain.

"Well, if your kidneys fail, which can happen, you would need a kidney transplant. Usually siblings are a perfect match, and they can give you one of their kidneys, but if you keep punching Peaches, she probably wouldn't give you one of hers, and then you would have to go on the transplant list, which is really long, hoping that some stranger would be a perfect match and give you one of their kidneys. I think your odds are better with your sister . . . so keep that in mind before you punch her again."

"Did you have to have a kidney transplant when you went to the emergency room? Did you almost die?" Peaches inquires.

"No, I had a kidney stone from the steroids they were putting in my back, and I didn't almost die, but the pain was so bad I was praying for death, until they gave me some medicine."

"Mom says that you really could have died from the car hitting you. I'm glad you didn't, because you're the only teenager who's friends with us," Candy says.

I love that they think I'm a teenager, although I'm afraid it might have been nothing to do with my youthful appearance and more to do with my immature attitude.

"I'm glad I didn't die, too. I don't know what you'd do without me. What do you say we go get some ice cream and watch some more heroin addicts?"

"Can we get double scoops dipped in chocolate?" Peaches pleads.

"Ummmm . . . I don't know. Will you give your sister a kidney if she promises not to hit you?" Peaches nods with a giggle.

"And Candy, do you promise not to punch your sister again?"

"Yes . . . promise," Candy says, crossing her heart.

"Well, then, I think there are double-scoop chocolate-dipped cones in your future."

"Yay!" they scream in unison, beginning to run down the street.

"Hey, guys, wait up, I can't run," I shout after them.

"Sorry, Hogan, we forgot," Candy says, running back toward me.

"Are you ever gonna get better?" Peaches asks.

"Of course I'm gonna get better. Now let's get that ice cream."

"I know . . . just checking," Peaches says, grabbing my hand.

They still believe in Santa Claus. They still believe in the Tooth Fairy . . . and just like me, they still believe I will get better. We might be the only three people who believe it, but that's enough for me. And with two cheerleaders named Peaches and Candy on my team, I'm sure to win.

"It's amazing that any of that ice cream made it into your mouth," I say, looking at the two of them with chocolate all over their faces and hands.

"Our heroin addict is gone," Candy whines.

"We can watch that homeless woman with all her stuff in a shopping cart," Peaches says optimistically.

"Yeah, I don't really want to watch a homeless person because there is a good possibility I could be one soon."

"Cool; can you be homeless in this park? 'Cause then we can visit you and have a sleepover," Peaches says with a giggle.

"Well done, Grasshopper, I think you're getting the hang of the sarcasm thing."

Mary Jane and Bud have beaten us home.

"Hello, and what did you all get up to?" Bud asks, as he is going through a shopping bag full of clothes. He has the best fashion sense of any straight man I know and picks out all of Mary Jane's and the kids' clothes, although Mary Jane can put together some really hideous combinations if he's not home to consult, but he himself always looks like an unmade bed.

"We went to the park and watched a heroin addict. Then we played for a while and Hogan told us about kidney failure, then we got ice cream and tried to find the heroin guy again, but we couldn't. Oh, and Hogan might be a homeless person in the park," Candy reports, as if she is giving a dissertation.

"Well, did you invite the heroin addict to show-and-tell? I'm sure your teacher would love that."

"Did you get loose with the credit card again?" I question, as he inspects the shopping bag.

"I went to the Martin Margiela sample sale and picked up a

few things for Mary Jane . . . and I got you these," he says, tossing a pair of pants at me.

"You got me something? Really?"

"Well, you deserve a gift. Try them on, they should fit—they look to be Barbie size," he says with a chuckle.

It's true, I've become the incredible shrinking woman on the PP Diet (Poverty and Pain), and I have about as many curves as a ten-year-old boy, but the thought of a new article of clothing has my little fashion heart jumping for joy.

"They fit," I victoriously shout as I exit the bathroom modeling my new pants.

"Good, now let's go shopping in Mary Jane's closet for you. She doesn't wear half the stuff anyway."

Bud works in the fashion business, and as an added bonus, designers are always giving him clothes. Since most of them are women's designers, Mary Jane reaps the benefits, and her closet is my version of Mecca; but being a stay-at-home mom, she is usually outfitted in jeans, and many of her designer duds have never seen the light of day.

Bud and I enter their bedroom, where Mary Jane is seated on the bed, rolling a joint. If joint-rolling were an Olympic event, Mary Jane would surely win a gold medal. Her skill and precision are awe-inspiring, and after years of practice, she has perfected it into an art form. Bud, on the other hand, could smoke for the *High Times* home team if he put his mind to it, but he's not the competitive type.

"Love, let's go through your closet and give Hogan some clothes," Bud says, opening the closet door.

Most women would stab a dagger in your heart at the mere

mention of parting with any of their fabulous frocks, but not Mary Jane. She simply smiles and says, "Okay." Generosity, cute kids, readily available pot—is it any wonder I love her?

Bud proceeds to rummage through the wardrobe like a personal shopper at Barneys, pulling articles out and tossing them on the bed. There is quite an impressive pile by the time he extracts his head from the closet. "Well, start trying them on," he instructs as he sits on the bed next to Mary Jane and lights the joint. And with that, I begin my fashion show for Cheech and Chong.

"No, take those off. You'll never get a date in those," Bud says, ixnaying the pants I just put on.

Note to self: For future reference, if you ever feel that your ass looks fat in something and you need an honest opinion, don't ask Mary Jane or another girlfriend, just ask Bud.

"Oh, that's a good one," he states, viewing me in a rose-colored corduroy Habitual jacket with a fake-fur-trimmed hood and the tags still on it. As I look in the full-length mirror, I feel instantly infused with a sensation that can only be described as a clothes-gasm. I haven't had a new article of clothing in over a year (and that includes underwear and socks). Life definitely sucks when a fashionista can't even buy a pair of socks. It's gotten to the point where I avoid walking down streets that have clothing stores on them, because it's far too torturous to even look at the window displays. It's not so sunny in Fashion-Depressistan, but things are finally looking up in a hand-me-down way.

"Are you sure you don't mind, Mary Jane? I mean, you haven't even worn it."

"No, take it. It looks better on you anyway," she states with a smile.

By the time we are finished, I have my pair of Margiela pants, a Habitual jacket, a Helmut Lang jacket, Jean Paul Gaultier pants, a black summer dress, and a huge grin on my face.

"You're staying for dinner, right?" Bud asks.

"Mary Jane's not cooking, is she?" I love her to death, but she could mess up the recipe for ice cubes.

"No, you're injured enough. We'll order in."

"Fuck off." Mary Jane laughs.

Mary Jane, Bud, Peaches, and Candy. Sounds like the members of a seventies hippie folk group. All I know is they're more than just friends—they're my family. And they just gave me the most precious gift of all: the gift of fashion—and a joint, to ease my aches and pains, for the road.

———————

A month later, I am at the office of Advocate, Legal Eagle, and Solicitor. I can't remember why they asked me to come in. Probably to sign papers . . . I'm always signing papers—power of attorney papers, lawsuit papers, financial loan papers; I think they have an entire file cabinet full of papers with my signature on them. I've already caught up and chitchatted with the receptionist, and now I'm sitting on the brown leather couch in the waiting room. I have developed a deep hatred for this couch, not only because it is ugly but, more important, because it is the most uncomfortable piece of furniture I have ever had the misfortune of sitting on. You'd think that since most of their clients are seriously injured they would have a more comfortable couch. It is so deep that even though I am five-ten, my feet can't touch the ground, and the back offers little to no support and seems to swallow me up. Quite frankly, the whole office could use a major interior-decorating face-lift, and I've voiced my opinion on this matter several times to Legal Eagle, but he just laughs. I guess they're more into the law than aesthetics, which is probably better for me in the long run. While I wait I mentally redecorate, adding a fresh coat of paint, a shabby-chic couch, a new coffee table, and a magazine selection from this calendar year.

"I haven't seen you in a while," Advocate's assistant says as she walks into the waiting room on her way to the bathroom to take her afternoon smoke break.

"Yeah, you must have been missing me horribly and suffering from withdrawals," I respond.

"No, I just thought we finally got rid of you." She laughs, exiting to her illegal smoking den. I adore her. She rules this office, and the lawyers practically genuflect when they see her. She always has a quick comeback or the perfect facial expression to let you know exactly what she thinks of something or someone. She's like the Lucille Ball of the office, and I love Lucy.

"He's waiting for you in the conference room," the receptionist says as she opens the door to the inner sanctum of the office.

"Hi, Hogan," Legal Eagle says as I enter the room. "You look awful."

"Well, I don't feel so good, either. Since No-Fault cut me off, I don't have physical therapy or my medications because I can't afford them."

"I can't believe you haven't been to physical therapy in three months and have been going without medications. Are you trying to ruin your case? The court and the jury don't care if you have no money or insurance. They will only hear 'She stopped going to physical therapy, and she stopped taking her medication. So she must be better.' You need to apply for Medicaid immediately."

Legal Eagle is a kind and gentle man, but I am clearly testing his patience.

"Isn't Medicaid for old people?"

"No, Medicare is for old people. Medic*aid* is for poor people." He smiles.

"Great, another government office. I can't wait."

I wish that when you got hit by a car or had some other cata-strophic accident, there were a book mapping out exactly what you should do, so you didn't feel like such a dumbass all the time. Why isn't there any communication between these government agencies and the general public? I have never seen a poster or ad on the subway saying, "You're hungry and have no money, apply for food stamps." "You're injured and can't work, apply for Social Security Disability." "You have no health insurance and are in-jured and poor, apply for Medicaid." It's as if they have created these programs to aid the needy, but they don't want to let the needy know about them. When I Googled "I am uninsured, poor, and injured. What should I do?" I got an entire page of health care providers that I can't afford and car insurance companies that I don't need. I might be a blonde, but even I know that's wrong. Thankfully, Legal Eagle eventually points me in the right direc-tion of the red tape.

The tiny Medicaid office is packed with mothers and crying chil-dren. I take a seat next to the only other childless woman in the waiting room, who is intently reading a book. It's going to be an eternal wait, and the two-year-old throwing a temper tantrum is not helping matters. God, this kid has some lungs and is the best argument for birth control I've ever heard. I inch forward slightly in my chair to see what the angelic-looking woman with the pixie haircut sitting next to me is reading, in an attempt to distract myself from thinking horrible thoughts about a toddler.

"Oh, you're reading Lance Armstrong's book. Are you a cyclist?" I ask feebly in hopes of striking up a conversation. She pauses for a moment and then raises her head from her book. "No, but I have cancer."

I feel completely awkward having stuck my foot in my mouth and flounder for something to say, but can only come up with a murmured apology. After a second I regain my composure, and I get her story. She is thirty years old, and for the first time in her adult life she had managed to get enough money together to get health insurance, because her employer doesn't offer it. After a month she went to her gynecologist for a routine exam, and they found a lump in her breast. Two weeks later she was diagnosed with stage-three breast cancer. The insurance company decided that it was a preexisting condition and won't cover her treatment. Medicaid is her only hope now to cover her treatment. "I know the insurance company doesn't care if I live, but I care. I'm only thirty . . . I'm not ready to die."

My head is swimming with outrage and questions, and my heart aches for this woman and the life-threatening situation she finds herself in, through no fault of her own. I don't tell her what has brought me here to this Medicaid office because it doesn't matter. What matters is that I'm here to listen. We might be strangers, but for this one brief moment in time, we are interconnected, and even though all I can offer her is kindness and my ear, I think in some small way it's helping.

They finally call my number, and I go back to meet my case-worker in her cubicle. She is a middle-aged woman who bears a striking resemblance to Maya Angelou.

"So, Hogan, why are you here?" she asks.

I begin to tell her my story but immediately burst into tears. I have become the public assistance crier. I'm not sure if I'm crying for myself or for the woman in the waiting room . . . or am I crying for all of us?

"Don't cry. You've done nothing wrong. This is not your fault," she says in a comforting way. Strangely, it's the first time that anybody has said that to me, and it makes me feel better. Maybe all this time I have been blaming myself for everything that has happened. After all, I asked the universe for a change. I was the one complaining about my waitressing job, the one who chose the unstable career path of an actor, and ultimately the one who didn't have health insurance. She hands me a box of tissue and continues to ask her questions.

"Are you married?"

"No. I have enough problems."

"Children? Let me guess—you have enough problems," she says with a warm smile.

"Exactly." I laugh through the tears.

"I will submit your outstanding medical bills, and we'll see if Medicaid will cover any of those. You will receive a Medicaid card in the mail in about a week. But should you need any immediate medical assistance, you can go right to the emergency room."

"Thank you for being nice to me."

"I'm just doing my job," she replies.

"You'd be surprised how many people that work in these places don't feel it's their job to be nice to people."

She receives my compliment with all the grace and elegance of the woman that she resembles. And then she reaches across her desk and grasps my hand. "You take care of yourself, Hogan."

And in that one brief moment, I feel protected, loved, and in the presence of something spiritual. Maybe some would call it God, in which case I hate to break it to the bigots of the world, but God looks a hell of a lot like Maya Angelou . . . and she is beautiful and kind.

~~~~~~~

After the Medicaid office, I can't seem to get the woman from the waiting room out of my head, so I need to cheer myself up with some retail therapy. Of course, these days retail therapy means food stamp shopping.

I walk down the grocery store aisles slowly, admiring all the food I can't afford. The Amy's organic roasted vegetable pizza is staring at me through the glass of the freezer, topped with marinated shitake mushroom, roasted red peppers, sweet onion, and marinated artichoke hearts. The picture on the box is making my mouth water at the memory of biting into a steaming hot piece. The veggie burgers are teasing me on a nearby shelf in the frozen foods section; how nice they would taste on a toasted bun with a slice of onion and ketchup, and a side of German potato salad sprinkled with fresh dill. The delicate bottle of truffle oil is looking decadent and the mere thought of it lightly drizzled over wild mushroom risotto is making my stomach growl. Just to torture myself a little more, I am perusing the prepared foods, which are looking exceptionally fresh and fun: sautéed spinach with garlic and toasted pine nuts; vegan lasagna cut into hearty portions, dripping with tomato sauce; raw kale salad with kalamata olives and avocados, shimmering under the lights of the store. But people on food stamps aren't allowed to buy prepared foods. Which is a stupid, nonsensical rule. If I were still on the model diet of coffee and cigarettes, sticking to my food stamp budget would be a breeze, but starvation is only cute on the young and stupid, and I unfortunately require food, especially since I seem to have come down with a case of that horrible disease called No-Ass-At-All. People talk about "junk in the trunk," but I don't even think I have a trunk anymore. So, needless to say, it's time to carb load with some pasta.

I'm feeling kind of fancy, sort of like a food stamp Martha Stewart, so I think it will be penne arrabbiata (spicy tomato sauce), a little green salad with beans (for protein), and a baguette to make bruschetta, which, of course, requires fresh tomatoes. With the tomatoes, I have reached my two-day budget limit of $9.40, but I can make this one meal last, and it's a balanced two-day feast. I'm really proud of myself every time I live within the confines of my circumstances and still manage to be healthy. That being said, I would love to challenge all the politicians currently debating health care reform or budget cuts on food stamps to only eat $4.70 worth of food a day for six months, because I bet my nonexistent ass that they wouldn't last three weeks. Maybe when I get better I'll do a cooking show called *$4.70 and Healthy* for all my welfare brothers and sisters. It will, of course, only focus on dinner, because for that amount you can't possibly expect breakfast or lunch. No, one meal a day is all we can afford, so we best make it a good one. I will also tackle subjects like, What the hell are you supposed to do if you can't buy prepared food on food stamps, and you don't have a kitchen or even a hot plate? I foresee a lot of sandwiches in that segment.

I am pulled out of my daydream of being a Food Network star by the cashier. "How would you like to pay?" he asks in a monotone.

"Food stamps."

"Slide your card and punch in your pin number." He checks his screen. "Try again. It's saying you punched in the wrong number."

The panic is setting in—what is my number? 6532 or 2356 or 8625? I can hear my neurologist's voice in my head: "It could take up to a year and a half for the swelling of your brain to go down and to determine if there is any permanent damage." My memory loss is still a nightmare, but I have never forgotten my food stamp number. Come on, Hogan, I tell myself, get a grip . . . you know this number. I take my best guess and punch in the numbers again.

"Nope, wrong. It's saying your card is declined now. Would you like to pay cash?" he asks with a smirk.

I look in my wallet to find a whopping twenty-five cents and a maxed-out credit card. "I'm sorry, I don't have any money," I whisper in the hopes that no one will hear me.

The look on his face is one of utter disgust. "Hmm . . . well, could you put the groceries back on the shelves for me?" he says loud enough for all to hear.

I refuse to give him the satisfaction of seeing me cry. I gather up my groceries and, as I turn around to put them back on the shelves, I try to avoid the pity-filled gazes in the line of people that has formed behind me, their shopping carts laden with food that they can pay for. Their quiet judgment is palpable, and I think I can hear their thoughts echoing in my head—*Poor thing . . . Loser . . . How pathetic.* As I put the groceries back in their proper places on the shelves, I feel an overwhelming sense of defeat and an overwhelming desire to go back up to the register and call the cashier a dicktard.

I arrive home to find my food stamp pin number, which is sadistically hung on the refrigerator with a magnet that reads, "Anyone who lives within their means suffers from a lack of imagination. Oscar Wilde." I stare at the number: 4365. It is as if I have never seen it before. It doesn't sound familiar at all, and I have been using it at least five times a week for more than a year.

Armed with my number, I decide to do a repeat performance at another grocery store. But again, my card is declined. It is now five p.m. on Friday and the welfare offices are closed. I will have to make do with whatever I have in my kitchen until I can sort out the food stamp debacle on Monday.

What would Martha do in a situation like this? I have ketchup, mustard, and sticky rice. You know what Martha would do? Martha would say, "Fuck this. I'm going to Nobu for dinner." I, on the other hand, have decided to go for the rice and ketchup combo, which is going to make for a rather monotonous and unappetizing three-day culinary experience, but if rice for every meal was good enough for Confucius, it's good enough for me, although Confucius probably didn't mix it with Heinz. He was, after all, the BC dude who said, "With coarse rice to eat, with water to drink and my bent arm for a pillow, I still have joy in the midst of all these things." I'm not sure I would call it joy, but I do have a pillow and condiments.

CHAPTER TEN

A Girl's Guide to What to Wear to the Welfare Office

After a weekend diet that would have made poor Karen Carpenter proud, I have come to the conclusion that man cannot live on rice alone; but it is Monday, and in honor of my growling stomach, I am going to DJ a little Monday-morning mix to get this day started right. Of course, the Carpenters are up first with "Rainy Days and Mondays Always Get Me Down," then "Manic Monday" by the Bangles, and finally "I Don't Like Mondays" by the Boomtown Rats. I had to go way back, old-school style, to come up with Monday songs. Note to musicians: Can someone please write a happy song about Mondays? 'Cause at the beginning of the week some of us need to turn a hungry stomach and frown upside down, and you guys are depressing the shit out of me, and as shocking as it may seem, the band Happy Mondays don't have one fucking song about Mondays.

On a high note: I have the food stamp office to look forward to and an outfit to plan. I should really write a book. It could be called *A Girl's Guide to What to Wear to the Welfare Office*. It'll be for the fashion-forward girl on public assistance. Kind of a *Sex and the City* meets *My Left Foot*. Some of the fashion tips I will cover:

1. When choosing an outfit for the welfare office, wear something that you haven't worn in a while so that it feels a little shiny and new. Hey, you're broke, and the price is right. Now, that's what I call bargain shopping.

2. If you are going to wear a skirt, make sure you have tights on, because those waiting room chairs have seen a lot of mysterious fluids over the years.

3. If your shoes are looking as tired and worn as you feel, give them a shine; it's like Botox for footwear.

4. Never wear yellow to the food stamp office, because when paired with the fluorescent lights, you'll look jaundiced, which is never a cute look.

5. Bring sunglasses for your exit from any public assistance office. Pretend that your future is so bright that you need to wear shades. They will also come in handy if you don't want to be recognized. You are the (welfare) queen, after all.

6. You might feel that you are in mourning for your present situation, but you don't have to look like you're going to a funeral. Wear colors and steer clear of dressing in all black. Life is depressing enough.

7. Spray a little of your favorite perfume on a scarf that you can carry in your purse, just in case the person sitting next to you

hasn't discovered deodorant or their baby's diaper is well overdue for a change. It's like your own personal gas mask.

8. Don't wear any T-shirts with food drawn on them (such as a cupcake or ice cream) to the food stamp office. People are hungry and that's just cruel—not to mention, someone might bite that dessert appliqué on your tit.

9. Only wear waterproof mascara to any welfare office. The hours of waiting may bring you to tears, and you don't want to look like a raccoon.

10. And, last but not least, have a motto for the day. My motto for today is, "Nothing says I have a brain injury and could possibly starve to death like Marc Jacobs." Come up with your own and make it silly.

I think this could be huge. Oprah will pick it for her book club, and we will become such good friends that I'll just call her O. I'm thinking *New York Times* bestseller, front window of Barnes & Noble, and a feature article in *Vogue*. I will, of course, wear my most stylish neck and back brace on the cover, and maybe even lean on my cane. It will start a fashion revolution among welfare recipients across the country, wearing their Sunday best to perk up the drab government offices and make themselves feel a little better. Like the L'Oreal campaign so eloquently puts it, "Because I'm worth it." I think it's so easy to forget that when you're down-and-out. You are worth the effort. Dress as if you are the lead in your own movie. You might currently feel that you're starring in that tragic Darren Aronofsky film *Requiem for a Dream,* but when you put on the right outfit, you'll feel like you've been dropped into the makeover scene from *The Devil Wears Prada*. Well, at least that's how I feel right now in my Marc Jacobs blue, circa-1960s-looking dress. It might be five years old, but I'm into recycling these days. So bring it on, food stamp office.

—————

The brief notice on the building door reads, *The food stamp office has moved. We are now located at 12 W 14th St.* Call me crazy, but it might be nice to inform people via mail, phone, or carrier pigeon that you have relocated your office so those who have painfully dragged their hungry, starving selves all the way to the wrong location don't feel the need to kick your vacated building with their ballet-flat-wearing foot. Ouch! Okay, note to self: The next time you are angry and generally over everything, think twice before booting a concrete building, Einstein. That foot was practically the only thing working on your body. I quickly look around to see if anyone has witnessed my Naomi Campbell impression, but much to my delight, none of the suits shuffling off to work seem to have noticed my one-way fight with said inanimate object . . . or if they did notice, they don't care. New Yorkers don't shock easily.

Time to regroup, reload, and move 'em out. I can be at the new office in twenty minutes if I limp at a good clip.

Hi-ho, hi-ho . . .

It's off to the new food stamp office we go.

Okay, that was lame even by my standards. I think I'm a little loopy after three days of ketchup rice. This ditty is running on loop in my head, and it's making me think of apples. (Of course I'm anything but Snow White, more like the wicked, hungry bitch-witch.) My stomach is crying out in agony, and this walk is proving to be torturous. I have already passed two Starbucks, and quite frankly I would give my left tit for a chai tea and a bagel, and I am rapidly approaching a food cart on the corner. The smell of the cooking lamb for the gyros is making my 100 percent vegan self salivate like a begging dog at the dinner table. I'm hungry in a feed-the-children-infomercial way.

My ex-boyfriend and I used to come home drunk after a night out and watch infomercials. One night I ended up purchasing a pasta maker, and not only the pasta maker but the five extra attachments, because at two in the morning, jacked up on the jackass juice, I was positive that I would not only make every kind of pasta imaginable but also bread sticks and bagels. Yeah, that never happened. I used the thing once, and it became the most expensive piece of artwork in my apartment. My boyfriend, on the other hand, turned into Angelina Jolie, supporting ten kids through Feed the Children. I thought his philanthropy was charming until we broke up and he moved out, leaving me to support his kids. In the memo line of every check I wrote to Feed the Children I would put a little note, like, "Your American dad is a deadbeat." Maybe I should have sent them the pasta maker, too. What is that old saying . . . Give a man a fish? . . . or is it, Teach a man to fish? Whatever . . . but I bet they would have made a hell of a lot more pasta and bread sticks than I did. Let this be a lesson: Drinking can lead to impulse buying and children that you didn't plan on supporting.

Crap! I've just made it to Union Square, and as luck would have it, the farmers' market is in full swing, which is a vegetarian paradise, and cruel and unusual punishment right now. The only thing worse would be ending up at the Barneys warehouse sale naked and penniless. All the produce seems to have been perfectly arranged by a food stylist, as it glistens in the early-morning sun. The beets have a deep earthy color, the tomatoes are a vibrant red, and the mesclun is meticulously misted with a light spray to bring out the different shades of green. This is food porn at its finest, and I so desperately want to be the fluffer. Easy, Traci Lords. I am weak, though, and take a moment to check out the freshly baked bread. Bread is my favorite food group. The seven grain with the oats scattered across the top, the sourdough with the golden crust, and the foccacia lightly drizzled with olive oil are just begging to be eaten. I still find it hard to believe that people go on that Atkins Diet that restricts carbs. What's the point in living if you can't have bread and pasta? In L.A., they don't even give you a bread basket when you go out to dinner unless you beg for it, and then the Barbie-looking girls at the other tables stare at you in disbelief, as if you were shooting heroin in the middle of the restaurant. They're a little scared of food out there.

"Can I help you?" the woman behind the bread counter asks.

"No, just looking. I'm on Atkins and visiting from L.A.," I respond in my best Valley Girl voice, and walk away while she still has the bemused expression on her face. I am so hungry, I think my stomach is digesting itself, and it's making some rather embarrassing sounds.

What the hell am I doing? I need to stop this torment and get the fuck out of here. Just walk. Walk by the jams and jellies, Hogan. Walk by the apples and peaches, walk by the homemade pretzels . . . wait, stop . . . rewind . . . the pretzel stand has a bowl of samples out. Eu-fucking-reka.

Now, when one is sampling, one needs to give the appearance that one is in the market to buy. One must not appear to be a

gluttonous starving pig; one must be a lady and only take one . . .
okay, maybe two . . . on second thought three. I now have three
large pieces of pretzel with sea salt in my mouth, and it's a rather
dry and crunchy situation. The bearded, ponytailed dude looming
behind the counter is looking pretty crunchy, too, in a stuck-in-
the-sixties kind of way.

"Can I help ya?" he asks in a monotone that makes me want
to ask him to pass the doobie.

"Do you ha any watah?" I question, with pretzel flying out of
my mouth.

"No, man, just pretzels," he responds. There are mushy pretzel
bits now lodged in his beard, and I decide to abort before he notices. And just like that I have scored a nutritious, slightly unbal-
anced breakfast of three pretzel pieces for free.

"Spare any change?" a panhandler asks as I cross the street.

"I'm sorry, I don't have anything." And unlike many New Yorkers he will encounter today, I'm not lying.

Come to think of it, I haven't seen my favorite panhandler-
slash-homeless guy, Sam the Man, since my accident. Sam the Man
used to panhandle outside this place I worked. He was amazing to
watch. The sidewalk was his stage, and he knew all the celebrities
who frequented the place on a first-name basis. He'd ask about
their significant others, or how sales were going for their latest
movie or record, and then he'd put out his cup. I remember one
night, after work, I asked him how much he had made that night,
and he had made double what I had waitressing for eight hours. I
said, "Give me that cup; I'm making a career change." He then
turned to another person on the street, "Can you spare any change?
This is my wife, and she's really high-maintenance." The guy put
ten dollars in the cup. I didn't take the money, of course, but we

laughed so hard that we cried. We became friends, and when I would get a new job, he would magically be working the sidewalk outside (as long as it was below Fourteenth Street—he's a downtown guy). Many nights he would walk me home after work just to make sure I was safe, and it was usually the best conversation of my evening. He was always invited to all my birthday parties, and although he never showed up, he invariably had a little present for me the next time I saw him. One year he gave me a men's gold ring. I'm pretty sure it was stolen, but it's the thought that counts. Anytime I run into him I can't help but stop and gab for at least fifteen minutes, no matter who I happen to be with, so he knows my mother and brother and most of my friends, and they all adore him just as much as I do. But my favorite Sam the Man times are when I take him out to lunch, and for that one hour he's just like any other person out for a meal with a friend.

I hope he's okay. I worry about him, but the next time I run into him, boy do I have a lot to catch him up on, although he might have to take *me* out to lunch.

The new food stamp office is bigger than the old one, but it still must have the same interior decorator, whom I imagine is named Countess-Depress-the-Fuck-out-of-Me. On the bright side, the small school desks have been replaced by neon blue plastic chairs, institutionally lined up in four rows. It's packed to the gills, and everybody looks equally miserable, with the promise of an eternal wait. Luckily for me, I'm not applying for food stamps. I'm already a card-carrying member, so I'll be in and out of here and food shopping in no time, once they kindly undecline my card.

"Hello, I punched in the wrong pin number, and my card has

been declined," I say to the woman at the front desk who bears an uncanny resemblance to a cranky pit bull.

"Take a numbah an wait to be called," she responds without looking up.

"But I have a card already, it's just not working."

She has now looked up with one hand on her hip and the other pointing at me. "I *said*, take a numbah an wait to be called."

I can feel the blood rushing to my head. My immediate reaction is anger; who the hell does she think she is talking to people like that? Does it make her feel superior? I want to yell, "You work for Health and Human Services, and I'm a human and I expect some service, bitch." But that approach probably won't get me very far, so I take a number . . . number eighty-six, and settle in for a long wait, being that they are now on number five.

I try to move my chair to get more comfortable, and after several attempts, I realize that it's nailed to the floor. You can't be too careful around us poor people; we might try to steal your neon blue furniture.

Eating in food stamp offices should be outlawed. It's like having a drink at an AA meeting. I would like to make a citizen's arrest on the five-year-old sitting next to me devouring a bag of peanuts. Don't they teach children to share these days? Said five-year-old is laughing at the huge growl my stomach just made. I wasn't aware that starvation came with such noisy and embarrassing sound effects. I stick my tongue out at the kid 'cause I'm mature like that. He laughs again and swallows some air and lets out the largest burp ever to emerge from such a tiny body. It's impressive. I've always been rather in awe of people who can make themselves burp on cue; it's a talent that I never mastered, and not for lack of trying.

I wonder what it's like for a child to be in one of these places . . . or for his mother, who has drifted off to sleep in the chair next to him, knowing that she needs help feeding her adorable burping-champion son. I hope he is oblivious to the thick cloud of depression and desperation that is blanketing this waiting room. I want him to believe that he can be anything: an astronaut, a doctor, or maybe even the president . . . yes, definitely the president. I think this country would be in much better shape if we had a president who had experienced firsthand the struggles of poverty and what it is like. Look at me, dreaming that some poor Latino kid will rise like a phoenix out of this mess of red tape and food stamp waiting rooms to become someone, someone important, who can make a difference, because I don't have the naivete to dream for myself anymore. My life before the accident seems like a distant memory. The hopes and plans I had for the future are gone, and now I am just some woman who is begging for the privilege to eat four dollars and seventy cents' worth of food a day. I am tired in a way that is indescribable. I wish I could go to sleep—maybe forever, I sometimes think, in the really bad moments, like right now.

When I was around the age of the boy sitting next to me, I remember being terrified before going to sleep that I wouldn't be able to wake up, that I would somehow get stuck in the dream world. My mother told me that if I ever felt like I was stuck in a dream, I should pray to my guardian angel, and she would guide me back to the real world. This simple little trick helped quell my childhood fear, and now here I am, an adult, stuck in a nightmare, and there is no angel to guide me back.

"Fireman, fireman," the five-year-old exclaims with glee. So much for my presidential plans for the kid. Still, at least it's a noble profession. "Fireman," he says again, pointing toward the entrance.

I look in the direction he's pointing, and sure enough, there are five of New York City's bravest entering the waiting room in full gear.

"Folks, no need to panic. We got a call about the smell of gas, so we're just going to check it out," a tall, dark-haired, and tragically cute firefighter announces.

Great, as if the food stamp office isn't bad enough, it could now possibly be a gas chamber. I do actually feel a little light-headed, but that could be due to the fact that I've only eaten ketchup rice and three pretzel pieces in the past four days. The little boy is eager to jump out of his chair and aid the firefighters who are investigating, but his mother, who has woken up, is having none of that and is firmly scolding him in Spanish. The pit bull behind the front desk is completely unfazed by the possibility of asphyxiation and is continuing to do whatever it is that she does. For most of the room, having the firefighters here is a little bit of entertainment to break up their long monotonous wait, but to me, it is a source of embarrassment—they are "outsiders." I'm sure none of them are on food stamps, and I don't want them intruding. This is "our" space, I think, suddenly protective of my welfare family and our neon blue haven.

Finally, after fifteen minutes, they have solved the problem. It was not a gas leak after all, just a rotting sandwich in the garbage can. And with that, I have my first laugh in a while—who throws out food in a food stamp office?

My future president has left me, but he waved good-bye and gave me a parting burp on his way out. His chair has been filled by a thirtysomething woman, with fingernails that I am transfixed by. They're actually more talons than fingernails. Each one has a pastel design painted on the top, and her two middle fingers each have a tiny blue rhinestone attached to the tip of the nail. I want to ask her if that's how she flips someone off in style, like a bejeweled "Fuck you," but she's busy feverishly texting, and I get the feeling that she's telling whomever it is to fuck themselves without her rhinestone single-digit salute. I don't know how she can text with those things. I'm quite positive that I couldn't do anything with nails like that, except maybe put my eye out. She clearly has been keeping them maintained, despite whatever hardship has brought her to this office. Before the accident I might have looked at her and thought, "How can she be concerned with such frivolous things when she's asking the government for assistance?" But now that I have stood in the same welfare lines and gotten dirty looks in the grocery store when using the same food stamps, I get it. You have to hang on to something from your old life to make your present situation more bearable. I am sure her nails are like my clothes are to me: one little piece of indulgence and style that is sometimes all she has to make herself feel better when everything else is falling apart.

Each one of these government offices seems to have the same clock, which was clearly stolen from my grade-school classroom. The round frame, the white face with the black hands and numbers, and just like the ones in grade school, they seem to move incredibly slow. For the past three hours I have been watching it creep along. It's the waiting that's hard; it gives everyone too much time to think. I can see it on the others' faces, too. We are different ages, different sizes, different genders and colors, but we are all quietly asking the same questions: When will it get better? When will it get easier? And none of us know if it ever will.

The woman to my right is still texting, and the man on my left is doing a scratch-off lottery ticket. He pauses before he scratches each box off with a faded penny, as if he is making a wish, and I hope, for his sake, that it is his ticket out of here.

"Numbah eighty-six," the pit bull bellows like a drill sergeant.

"Coming," I shout. It's taking me a second to get upright, as my feet have gone numb from sitting so long, and my back takes a while to straighten out . . . just one of the many joys of being a marginally functioning cripple.

"Hi. As I was telling you before, my card—"

"Well, you're gonna have to tell me again. All you people's stories sound the same," she snaps back.

Don't react, Hogan, just bite your tongue, I repeat silently as I strain to get words out. "I have a brain injury, and I used the wrong pin number because I couldn't remember it, and now my card is declined and I haven't been able to get food for four days."

"Le me see ya card." I hand her my card and she punches my number in the computer and, without looking at me, she tosses it back on the desk. "Well, it says your card is fine." And then she looks out to the crowd. "Numbah eighty-seven."

"But it's not working. When I try to use it, it says it's declined."

She turns her eyes to me and stares in my face and bellows again, "Numbah eighty-seven."

"Will you please check your computer again?" I beg.

"Will you move aside, so I can help this otha person?" she growls while waving me off.

"But you haven't helped *me*."

"If you don't move, I'll call security!" she shouts while gesturing to the uniformed, rather large guard at the entrance.

I then do what any rational adult would do: I burst into tears, right as number eighty-seven is telling her story. I shuffle out of the office on Fourteenth Street and continue crying—actually, crying is an understatement. I am sobbing like I have never sobbed before, and I can't stop. I have reached my breaking point, the end of my tether. Whatever you want to call it, I am there. I can't take it anymore: the lack of humanity, constant pain, doctors who can't fix me, memory loss, food stamps, disability, Medicaid, lawyers, poverty. I'm done. I don't want this life. I find myself turning almost without thought and walking toward the Brooklyn Bridge—the bridge I used to run across when I was healthy—and with each sobbing step I take I am more determined and convinced that this is the only way out.

I've had a few friends end their own lives, and I didn't understand how things could get so bad that someone would want to kill themselves. But now I understand. When you wake up and it's dark and you know that there is no hope that today the clouds will drift away because you've been hanging on every day, for days, months, maybe years, and the sun never comes. When you've been down so long that a smile feels wrong. You're not fun anymore; all you talk about is your misery and your pain, and people listen (sometimes), but you watch their eyes gloss over in a distant stare. They can't help you; nobody can, not even yourself. You dress each day in something you used to love, praying that it will magically transport you back to a time when you were happy, but it never does. You've stopped dreaming, you've stopped hoping, and you've stopped living. So this final act will merely be a formality. Finally, it will stop. Finally, I will have peace. Finally, there will be relief. I understand now, my friends, and I am coming to meet you on the other side of this cesspool that's called life.

The salt from my tears is stinging my skin, my nose is running down my face, and I am invisible to the people I walk by on the street, on my final march of defeat. I need to call my mother and say good-bye. I don't want her to find out from some stranger at the coroner's office. That would just be cruel. My hand trembles dialing my cell phone, and as she picks up the phone, my sobbing is now wailing. I don't even know what I'm saying, it's just flying out of my mouth like a fever dream, and my mother is caught off-guard. "Sweetheart, is that you? Hogan, honey, I can't understand you. Slow down . . . it's okay, just breathe . . . I know . . . I know, it's hard . . . but it will get better . . . I know it doesn't seem that way right now, but . . . What do you mean you're walking to the bridge? Sweetheart, you're not thinking clearly . . . I don't think that . . ."

She's clearly panicked now, but I feel resolved, and she is not changing my mind. I am done . . . done with it all. I try to tell her this and she cuts me off and in her best stern-mother voice says, "Now, you are going to be quiet for a minute and just listen to me. You lived through what should have been a fatal accident. What if you jump off the bridge and you live and you're in worse shape than you are now? Did you think about that? I mean, things haven't been exactly going your way, and even if you are success-ful, I'll dig you up and kill you again. So, I think you should pull your head out of your ass now and go home and call that food stamp office and maybe you'll get a human being on the phone."

My tears have now turned into laughter. I don't know why this is striking me so funny, but it is. When she gets angry, she gets kind of gangster, and I have always found it hysterical. She's right; with the way things are going, I probably wouldn't be successful in my suicidal endeavors. I have always appreciated some good gallows humor. It feels good to laugh, and for the first time in a while it feels good to be alive.

"Jesus, you can't scare me like that. Now you go straight home and call me when you get there."

As I hang up the phone, I stand still for a minute in the middle of the sidewalk, as New York bustles around me, and I take in a deep breath and quietly thank whoever might be listening that I called my mom and she said exactly the right thing at the right time. I would have jumped if it wasn't for her, and it scares me that I have allowed myself to get that low.

"You might wanna walk. It is called a sidewalk," a random guy yells as he's trying to get past me.

"Oh, go jump off a bridge," I retort with a laugh.

⸻

I do manage to get someone on the phone at the food stamp office, and not only was my card not going through because I couldn't remember my number, but when I got approved for Medicaid, my food stamp card was accidentally canceled. The woman on the phone tells me it happens all the time—it's a computer glitch. And it almost sent me off a bridge. Some glitch.

Since I have abandoned my bridge dive and am now back in the land of the living, I am going to have to find a way to get through this. When I was a kid, I liked to go to the beach and watch the surfers. I was mesmerized by the way they rode the vast ocean waves, like they were taming some wild beast. (Plus, they were cute.) One day I worked up the nerve to talk to one of them. I asked if he was ever scared about getting pulled into an undertow and drowning.

"No, dude, if you get pulled under, you have to go with it, and you'll eventually pop up to the surface, but if you fight against it, you'll drown. It's kinda like life," he answered with a sun-kissed smile.

"Really, you never get scared?"

He laughed. "Sure, I get scared sometimes, but then I just remember this." He showed me a button on his backpack that read, *The human race has one really effective weapon, and that is laughter.* "It's this dude, Mark Twain. He's pretty righteous," he said before departing with his board.

I think I finally understand what he was trying to tell me with all of his sixteen years of wisdom. Starting today, I will not let this drown me, I will stop fighting against it, and I will eventually surface. If I can just hang on until the trial, justice will be served and I will have the resources to get better. And until then I will laugh. Laugh at myself; try to find the humor in even the most difficult of situations. Now when someone asks, "What happened to you?" or says, "It's not often that you see a hot cripple" as I limp down the street, I will turn to them with a chuckle and respond, "I fell off my pole at Scores . . . stripping is a very dangerous profession."

It's a much better story than "I got hit by a car." That's so Oprah book club, so last year.

CHAPTER ELEVEN

Blanche DuLaw

It's not nice to laugh at the physically and mentally impaired—unless that person happens to be you, in which case it is acceptable and recommended. Laughter has been proven to improve one's health and stress levels (except of course if you are a comedian and then you apparently have a high probability of OD'ing Belushi-style). I'm sure I'm safe, since I am in no way a comedian, which is evident by the jokes I came up with today in honor of my newly adapted "a laugh or two a day keeps the bridge jump at bay":

1. Did you hear about the blonde who got hit by a car going forty miles per hour? She believed people when they told her that her looks could stop traffic.

2. Did you hear the one about the ex-model on food stamps? Food was a foreign concept to her, so she tried to mail a letter to Europe with them.

3. Did you hear the one about the blonde who had a brain injury? It happened when she tried to use it. If she'd only read the manual that said, "display model only."

Self-deprecation is the sport of the future. I mean, really, my life would make a great board game. It would be the anti-Monopoly. Players would each have a broken playing piece to move around the board, and instead of making money they would lose money. They would, however, acquire things with each move they make: neck braces, back braces, canes, and debt. And with each spin of the wheel, the arrow would make them move their broken piece to a new adventure, like the food stamp office or Medicaid, where they would pay with dignity chips. The winner is the one who acquires the most injuries, lands in the most government offices, and racks up the most debt. Macabre children the world over will put it on their Christmas wish lists, and Toys R Us will have a whole aisle filled with Totally Screwed, the board game.

I heard somewhere—either Oprah or that guy Deepak Chopra—that doing positive affirmations in the mirror helps you overcome obstacles, and the more you say them, the more they start to seep into your subconscious. So I have decided to perform my Choprah affirmations. If I understand this correctly, it is the equivalent of a private pep talk between you and yourself, so I am standing in my bathroom and looking at myself in the mirror. It's been a while since I really took a good look, and someone is looking a bit worse for wear. In my mind, my appearance was a lot better than this. I didn't have the deep circles under my eyes or the hollowed-out cheeks, which give me an overall gaunt effect. My complexion was glowing and not sallow, pasty, and drawn, and my roots weren't quite so white trash, because, of course, I haven't been able to afford salon visits or even at-home hair-color kits for months now. I need to give this lady in the mirror a talking-to because she's a little toe-up.

"Don't hate me because I'm beautiful, just hate me because I'm better looking than you are." Okay, Sybil, that was totally un-called for and verging on *Heathers*. You need to be nice. Let's try this again. "You look . . . pretty hot." God, I can't even say that with a straight face. It's more of a hot-mess situation. I think I need to rewrite the "I Feel Pretty" song from *West Side Story* to fit this state of undone.

> *I feel ugly*
> *Oh, so ugly*
> *I feel ugly and stupid and dull.*
> *And I envy*
> *Any girl who isn't me tonight.*

> *I feel lame*
> *Oh, so lame*
> *It's alarming how lame I feel.*
> *And so ugly*
> *That I barely believe I'm real.*

> *See the ugly girl in that mirror there:*
> *Who can that ugly girl be?*
> *Such an ugly face,*
> *Such an ugly shirt,*
> *Such an ugly smile,*
> *Such an ugly me.*

I'm not sure if this affirmation stuff is my style. The last time I tried to be New Age and ask the universe for a change it didn't exactly work out. On the upside, it is making me laugh at my unbelievable dorkiness, 'cause there is nothing cool about talking to yourself in the mirror.

Okay, let's give this one more shot: "You will get better. You will be healthy and happy again." Oh, that's a good one. Let's put that on rewind, and this time, say it like you mean it, sister. "You will get better. You will be healthy and happy again." And one more time just for shits and giggles. "You will get better. You will be healthy and happy again." Now let's write that on the mirror in your favorite red Chanel lipstick, just so you don't forget it, Little Miss Memory Loss. Move over, Choprah, there is a new self-help queen in town, and she is positively affirming all over the place.

It has been almost two years since the accident, but there is a light at the end of the tunnel with my rapidly approaching trial, where I will be suing for damages. I am, however, a bit worried that we haven't been able to track down my only eyewitness—the man who saw everything, whose description of what happened on the police report is exactly the same as mine. He is my ace in the hole, my slam-dunk . . . but he has disappeared. My lawyer has sent letters to him to no avail and left phone messages, which are never returned. And now we've had to hire a private investigator to track him down. Actually, we are on our second private investigator because the guy keeps moving across state lines. As soon as the investigator gets an address, he has already pulled a Houdini.

My injuries speak for themselves, but without this man to testify, it is just my word against the driver and passengers of the car
as to how the accident happened.

I have never needed anyone more in my life than I need this
stranger. I'm not asking for blood, I just need him to do the right
thing . . . to show up and tell the truth. But time is running out.

In the meantime, I have my first coaching session with Legal
Eagle for the trial. We will have these for the next couple of weeks
leading up to the trial to prepare me for what I can expect in the
courtroom.

Now, normally when you are involved in an automobile personal injury lawsuit, you are suing the driver. The driver's car insurance carrier has the obligation to pay up to its policy limits, but
in this case the driver took out one of the cheapest insurance
policies possible, with the most basic coverage, and then leased his
car to protect his personal assets. So I am suing the driver and the
leasing company, which means I am up against two legal teams in
the courtroom. In short, I need to train for this thing like a glad-
iator trains for the arena. I learned a fun little fact the other day:
Even though the car insurance carrier has the obligation to pay up
to its policy limits, a jury never hears the word *insurance* during trial. Mention of insurance is grounds for a mistrial . . . so I
have to erase that word from my vocabulary.

The oak table in the conference room at the office of Advocate,
Legal Eagle, and Solicitor is covered with the minutiae of my life
post-accident: There are detailed medical files from each one of
my doctors; emergency room reports; photos of the street where
the accident took place; photos of my bruised body; MRIs, x-rays,
and CAT scans; police and ambulance reports; documentation
from food stamps, Medicaid and Social Security Disability; and

my deposition. That's it; the past two years is contained on one table—all the trauma, all the pain, all the humiliation—and now I need to make these documents talk and to tell my story to a jury of my peers, so that Lady Justice can weigh and balance her scales, hopefully in my favor. I'm overwhelmed looking at all the papers. A lot of trees have been sacrificed in my wake since the accident; a lot has happened to me physically, emotionally, and financially, and I must say I am not looking forward to reliving every grue-some detail. But then I think of how much worse it must be for rape or assault victims, for instance, to have to dissect second by second their brutal attack, and I know that if they can step up to the plate in the name of justice and what is right, I can and I will, and I will draw strength from the people of this world who have faced far greater atrocities than I could ever comprehend.

I think I just had an "I am woman hear me roar" moment.

Legal Eagle is walking into the conference room carrying a yellow legal pad. I guess lawyers actually do write on those things (who knew?). He is wearing a charcoal gray suit; I'm guessing it's Brooks Brothers. I must say I do really appreciate that he is always dressed in a suit. Some of the others in the office wear jeans on occasion but not Legal Eagle, he's not really a jeans kind of guy.

"I've got some good news for you. The PI found your eyewit-ness yesterday and served him with a subpoena," Legal Eagle says nonchalantly.

"Halle-fucking-lujah."

By now Legal Eagle is used to my fondness for four-letter words and my propensity to try to create new ones. He finds it mildly amusing. "Now don't get too excited. We still don't know if he'll show up to court."

"Isn't it the law?"

"Well, not everybody obeys the law, but hopefully we'll hear from him soon."

I know he's just erring on the side of caution; he is, after all, a lawyer. But I'm not going to let him rain on my parade and the little bit of excitement in the vast wasteland of my life. This is one small step for me and one giant step toward justice. He's a little bit excited, too, I can tell; he just has a better poker face than I do.

"Let's get started," Legal Eagle says, taking a seat across the table from me and launching into a litany of questions.

"Back in the beginning of 2004, were you employed?"

"Where?"

"What were your duties?"

"On March fourth of that year, were you scheduled to work?"

"Now, you can't testify in great detail how the accident occurred, but in general, describe how the accident occurred."

I am firing off answers, but I pause on the last one to collect my thoughts for a split second, trying to figure out how to phrase it generally and not specifically. "You can't pause. It will read to the jury that you are unsure," Legal Eagle schools. Thankfully, my short-term memory is almost back to blonde status. I still get the awful stabbing headaches, but all the details of the accident are burned into my head, and as I describe it, I can almost see it, feel it, smell it, and taste it.

"You have a call on line one. It's the eyewitness," the receptionist announces over the intercom.

Oh my God. I am the luckiest girl on the planet right now. I mean this is better than unlimited free shopping at Bergdorf's, better than front-row tickets to Wilco concerts for the rest of my life, better than Johnny Depp naked in my bed . . . Okay, that last one is up for debate, but this is pretty fucking fantabulous. I think my Kismet and Karma cards are changing finally. I kind of want to get up on this table and do an Irish jig (I took Irish dancing in grade school and it's like dancing in a straitjacket—we micks have a strange idea of getting jiggy). But my geriatric spinal column will only let me entertain the idea for a nanosecond, so instead I just smile and let another "Halle-fucking-lujah" spring out of my ladylike lips.

Legal Eagle makes the universal symbol for "be quiet" as he picks up the phone. The man on the other end of the phone is yelling so loud that not only can I hear him but Legal Eagle has to put him on speakerphone to save his eardrum.

"You fucking leave me alone. I moved through three states to get away from you people. This is entrapment. If you think I'm going to show up in a courtroom so that bitch I used to be married to can have her way, you got another thing coming."

What the hell is he talking about? It sounds like he's worried that he's going to get busted for alimony or child support. This isn't Jerry Springer.

Legal Eagle is assuring him that there is no conspiracy; this is just about the accident. His face is growing increasingly red with frustration, and I am on the verge of tears.

"But I already told your investigator everything, and after he told me that she jumps in front of cars to make her money and her rich family is behind it, I even changed my story. He got it all on tape, and he promised me that if I did I wouldn't have to testify. I have to work!" he shouts.

The other side got to him first, pretending to be an investigator from our side. Told him lies about me, and then fed him what they wanted him to say and tape-recorded it. I am now officially crying. Who would be so vindictive? Was it the rich people who hit me, the leasing company, or the insurance company that hired this lying investigator? I guess it really is irrelevant who did it; all that matters is that with enough money you can buy history, too, and the person with the biggest checkbook wins. But Legal Eagle is not going down without a fight. "I'm the victim's lawyer; you spoke to the wrong investigator. The investigator you talked to works for the other side. This girl's life has been turned upside down. The accident has left her so injured that she hasn't been able to work. She has nothing; she's on food stamps."

"I find that hard to believe," the eyewitness laughs.

This is sending Legal Eagle into apoplexy. "Really? You find that hard to believe? She was a working stiff just like you are. What do you think would happen to you if you got hit by a car and couldn't work? You have a chance to do the right thing here. You were the only person who witnessed the accident. You're the only one who can help this poor girl."

He's having a very Erin Brockovich moment, minus the tits.

After several hours of yelling, conspiracy theories, and two hang-ups, the eyewitness has finally calmed down and agreed to testify for me—if we fly him and his Thai girlfriend in and put them up at a nice hotel. Christ, I'll supply the Ping-Pong balls at this point, as long as the guy shows up and tells the truth.

—————

The trial is set to start the day after tomorrow. I'm in my study den, otherwise known as the conference room, going over my deposition and medical records. Legal Eagle, on the other hand, is at the courthouse selecting the jury with the lawyers from the other side. Jury selection is no small feat, not only because these people determine the verdict of the case but also because it is rather difficult to find eight New Yorkers willing to sit in a courtroom all day without their computers and cell phones. I must admit that the one time I was called for jury duty I wore an anarchy T-shirt and sat in the corner talking to myself so I wouldn't get picked, and it worked. I'm kind of kicking myself for that right about now, and I'm a little worried that Legal Eagle is having to deal with smartasses like me, since he has been in jury selection for the past few days and has yet to find an acceptable jury. Hopefully, today will be the day.

I'm trying to stay as calm as I can; I feel a lot better since we found the eyewitness. With him to testify, my case is pretty rock solid, and Legal Eagle has decided that he will put him on the stand first.

Legal Eagle arrives back from the courthouse. "Well, I've got some good news and some bad news. Which do you want first?" he asks with a furrowed brow.

"Good, I guess."

"Well, we have six of our jurors, just two more to go."

"Well done, lawyer man . . . and the bad?" I question, fearing that maybe the eyewitness has had a change of heart.

"We got assigned to a judge . . ." He pauses.

This should be a good thing. I mean, we almost have a jury, and now we have a judge. I'm not seeing any problem, so I look at him with question marks in my eyes.

"Well, you might have read about her in the paper when she was arrested for drunk driving after ramming her car into a cop's car."

"You're kidding, right?" He is obviously not joking, as evidenced by the serious-as-a-heart-attack look on his face. "How can a woman who got arrested for drunk driving be the judge on a car accident case?" I shriek.

"I wish I were kidding."

Legal Eagle goes to confer with Advocate and Solicitor in hushed tones outside the conference room while I have a slight panic attack in the room filled with all the paperwork that documents what an utter disaster the past two years of my life has been, and now I can add Judge Lush to the mix.

On the plus side, we finally have a jury of eight law-abiding New Yorkers, and I am very grateful that they are willing to put their lives on hold to sit through my trial. Unfortunately, we have an issue with the settlement recommendation, which the judge is supposed to give based on her assessment of what the case is worth, in the hope that the two sides can reach a settlement before my case goes to trial. Judge Lush gave one number to my lawyer and another number to the other side that is significantly lower. I guess math is optional after a few drinks. She tried to forcibly suggest that we accept the lower number even after her egregious error, but we have politely declined and are proceeding with the trial that is set for tomorrow.

The eyewitness and his girlfriend have flown in and are safely at a very nice hotel enjoying room service, and my mother has flown in from California. The two of us are in my second home, otherwise known as the conference room. I am preparing for the trial, reading over my deposition; Mom, on the other hand, is reading one of her gossip magazines, or as she likes to call them her "learned journals."

"Sweetheart, I've been watching every *Law and Order* episode. I know all the legal jargon, and I think you should dress business casual for the trial. Everybody on *Law and Order* is always in business casual." Well, I guess she's been preparing for the trial in her own way.

"I'll keep that in mind," I respond with my head still buried in papers. All the information, all the facts, all the answers are just blurring into one big fog. I am overwhelmed, scared, frustrated, and in general stressed. I'm the one who got hit. I didn't hurt anyone; they hurt me. So why does it feel like I'm the one who's going to be on trial? Why am I the one who has to prove myself when I have done nothing wrong?

I have to believe that the judge will give me a fair trial. I'm sure that once we walk into that courtroom, she will be the consummate professional. Yes, she did get behind the wheel of a car while intoxicated, but people make mistakes, and I am sure that she probably faced a lot of adversity as a result of it, so hopefully she will be empathetic to the struggle and the pain that I have faced, and am still facing.

"That George Clooney is so cute. I think you should date him, honey. You two would be such a cute couple."

"Yeah, Mom, I'll get right on that. I'm sure he'd love to go out with a gimp on food stamps," I retort without looking up.

"Doesn't Britney know that they make shirts that cover your stomach?"

"Mom, I am trying to concentrate."

"I'm sorry, I'm just nervous and trying to make conversation."

We are both nervous wrecks, but Legal Eagle just arrived back from the courthouse, and he is dressed to impress in a navy blue suit. I hope he has some good news for us because I could use a little pick-me-up right about now.

"Any news?" I ask in a forcibly cheery way, as I fake a smile.

"I have never tried a case with this woman before, but she's living up to her crazy reputation. When I told her that we had finally found the eyewitness and that we had flown him in, she decided on the spot to bifurcate our case. Meaning she decided to split it in half, trying damages first and liability second. So this bitch—excuse my language—wants to try your case backward, which is never done. And when I explained to her that we didn't know if we'd be able to get the eyewitness back at a later date, because of his work schedule, she told me that was my problem."

"Well, this is just ridiculous. This would never happen on *Law and Order*," my mom exclaims.

Legal Eagle seems as frazzled and confused as we are, and Advocate and Solicitor have stopped into the conference room to commiserate. They are all trying desperately to keep our spirits up, but we all know that this is a bad situation. If anyone can turn this around, though, it's Advocate, Legal Eagle, and Solicitor, because they are the best and they are in it to win it . . . I want to shout "Go team," but I'm feeling so queasy that I'm afraid if I open my mouth I'll puke all over the place.

"Sweetheart, why don't we go outside and get you some air?" my mother suggests, clearly noticing the I-could-possibly-faint look on my face. She guides me out of the office with a death grip on my arm, down to the ground floor in the elevator and outside onto the street as Legal Eagle heads back to the courthouse.

The street is filled with people bustling by on their lunch breaks. Some talk into their cell phones, some are walking and talking with a friend, and I just saw one guy talking to himself. They all seem like they are on top of the world. I feel like the world is on top of me.

I am starting to feel light-headed. "Take some deep breaths, honey," my mom instructs. In, one, two, three. Out, one, two, three. In, one, two, three. Out, one, two, three. "Do you want me to walk to Starbucks and get you a chai?"

"No thanks," I answer.

"What? No chai? Are you dying?"

"Death would be a plus right about now. I must have been an axe murderer in a past life. Let's go back upstairs before I start punching happy people."

"Don't attack anyone, honey. You might end up with the same judge," she says with a nervous giggle.

My mother and I deal together well in stressful situations because we're the only ones who can put up with the other when the shit hits the fan. The past two years have been the most stressful thing we've been through, and I wouldn't have made it this far without her making me laugh when I needed it the most. She tries to be strong for me, but this has all taken its toll on her, and I can tell that she's barely keeping it together. I hate that I am putting her through this, but I am eternally grateful that she is here with me because I would probably kill anyone else.

Back in the four-wall prison of the conference room there are no windows to the outside world. Time seems to stand still here, and the only evidence that hours are passing is through the window looking out on the rest of the office. Legal assistants roaming past with files, the receptionist getting her first, second, and finally third coffee of the day, and Legal Eagle just arriving back from the courthouse yet again.

"You should probably sit down," Legal Eagle instructs as I stand to stretch my spasming back. "The judge has now decided to postpone your trial for two weeks because she has a funeral to go to."

"A funeral with a two-week after-party? Who died? Keith Richards?" I shout.

"This is fucking unbelievable." My mom sighs.

She's right. It is fucking unbelievable. Why is she doing this to me? I wish I could just switch judges, but Legal Eagle already explained that I can't. Judge selection is random, which means I am getting randomly fucked, and unfortunately you can only request a new judge if they do something illegal. Although what Judge Lush is doing is wrong, it is within the confines of the law. And even if you have a judge who does something illegal and you request a new judge, your case goes to the back of the line and it could be another year until a trial. I am acquiring an education in our judicial system that I never planned on . . . and it is offering me no comfort at all.

"We also lost two of our jurors because of this," Legal Eagle adds.

I am so angry I am ready to kick kittens, and I can tell that Legal Eagle is just as angry. We flew my eyewitness and his girlfriend in for nothing. So that's two roundtrip plane tickets, two nights in a fancy hotel, and a few nice meals that will all go on my tab. And if we are lucky enough to get him back for the liability half of the trial, we will have to organize and pay for it all again. My mother, on the other hand, will have to fly back to California and work for two weeks and then fly back for the trial. So that's two roundtrip plane tickets that she can't afford. And then there is me, who has already taken out two fifteen-thousand-dollar loans to pay bills and survive for the past two years, and the longer this trial drags on the higher the interest climbs, and I have about a hundred bucks to my name presently. Medicaid has cut off my physical therapy because I reached the max that they allow, and my back pain is still sending me on a downward spiral toward hell. And, just to add insult to injury, I am stuck with a judge who has to go to a two-week funeral. Maybe we could get a double burial because I want to die.

The two weeks pass like slow water torture, sitting in the conference room with Legal Eagle every day continuing to prepare for the trial. Describing that fateful evening over and over again, and verbally dissecting the pain I live with on a daily basis, have brought back my accident nightmares. I wake myself up most nights screaming, and now that my mother has returned for the trial tomorrow, I wake her up, too. It is, however, fair payback because the woman snores like a foghorn.

It's the crack of dawn (which to me means 9 a.m.), and I can hear my mom getting dressed in the living room. Between the snoring and the screaming neither of us got much sleep last night, but it's Sunday, which means that my mother is going to church to pray for my sorry ass. My mom laughingly refers to her worry praying as "going to talk to her imaginary friends," and my brother and I are her heathen children. Once we reached what she deemed the "age of reason" at twelve, she let us decide if we wanted to continue going to church on Sundays, and my brother and I determined that sleeping in was a far more spiritual experience.

So, other than the occasional Christmas Eve, I don't really darken the door of a church.

Today, though, I decide I should probably get up. It's really pointless to lie here any longer waiting for another night terror. Rolling onto my left side, I place my hands down and slowly rise onto all fours. I pause in this position for a moment, taking deep breaths and waiting for the spasming to subside a bit, and then I slowly walk my hands up the wall to a semistanding position. The pain survey says, "It's not going to be a great day." I wait for a moment until I can feel my feet a little bit more but eventually decide I'm about as good as I'm going to get on my old Novocaine legs.

I put on a Stella McCartney shirt (one must be stylish before the Lord) and grab a pair of pants, and slowly and carefully shuffle my way into the living room. My mom has seen my G-string-attired butt before, and I need to sit down on the couch to put my pants on.

"Honey, why are you getting dressed?" she asks while putting on her drugstore face, using the tiniest compact mirror ever to be used for makeup application.

"I'm coming with you."

"You're what?"

"I'm not taking any chances. On the off chance that there is any truth to your imaginary friends, I'm covering all my bases."

"You are aware that the crucifix might fly down and hit you over the head, and the church will probably burst into flames the minute you walk in the door, right?"

"Yeah, well, I'll just use you as a shield. Having an ex-nun for a mom has to be good for something," I retort.

"You're such a bitch." She laughs.

"Whatever, idol worshipper. Let's get moving, or they might lock you out of Heaven."

Okay, I'll admit I'm a hypocrite running off to church because I am so petrified of my trial tomorrow, but as they say in the big book, "Let him who is without sin cast the first stone." And if there is a God, I'm pretty sure he'll take a hypocrite, too . . . I mean church attendance has been down a little over the past few years, so he can't necessarily afford to be picky. That being said, I hope the holy water doesn't burn too bad . . . I think I'll make Mom test it first.

Finally, I am having my day in court. I am nervous but confident and dressed for success in a button-down Helmut Lang shirt, a V-neck dark blue sweater, and navy blue Marc Jacobs pants. It is a conservative, respectful, and overall nondescript outfit. Everything in my closet is too big on me these days, and even the size 2 pants I have on are hanging on me, but hopefully the sweater will camouflage my protruding bones.

The trial is set for ten a.m. sharp, so my mother and I arrive at the courthouse at nine thirty to meet Legal Eagle and pass through the metal detectors. There are so many uniformed officers that it resembles visiting day at Rikers.

"You ready?" Legal Eagle asks, walking up to greet us.

"Yes, good thing I left my machete at home."

"Now, when we go upstairs, there is no holding room for the jurors, so they will be sitting in the hallway outside the courtroom," Legal Eagle warns.

The elevator is crowded with legal types holding briefcases and shuffling in and out on different floors. "This is us," Legal Eagle eventually says, guiding us off the elevator. I can feel my stomach rising up into my throat, and the walls of my mouth are as dry as the Mojave. I have waited for this day for almost two years; sometimes the only thing that has kept me going is the promise that justice will be served. And now here it is: the light at the end of the tunnel, my chance to tell my story to a jury of my peers. The emotions that are running through me right now are overwhelming, and I am growing increasingly frustrated that my legs aren't working very well today, causing me to shuffle like a ninety-year-old down the hallway as the jurors stare at me. Not really my idea of a stellar entrance.

I have only seen courtrooms on TV. But much to my dismay, there are not separate desks with comfortable chairs for the plaintiff and the defendant to sit at. There are only long wooden benches that look like church pews, which is sure to be a painful experience for me. The empty chairs in the jury box will soon be filled, the large official-looking desk will soon have a judge behind it, and the witness box will soon have each one of my doctors individually testifying in it. They are set to go on the stand first today after opening statements. You have to pay your doctors to testify because they have to clear their surgical calendars, so that's twenty-seven-thousand dollars in doctors' testimonies. Yeah, not exactly bargain-basement prices.

The lawyers for the other side are chatting. The woman is in her late thirties and is wearing an ill-fitting skirt and heels that look to be half a size too small. She must have gotten up extra early this morning to curl her hair. The man, on the other hand, is in his fifties and is wearing a slightly rumpled suit, and I can tell by the manner in which he gestures and talks that he is the one who will be running their side of the show.

There are a few other people in the courtroom. One is a uniformed officer, one's probably the court reporter, and I'm not sure what job title the other one holds, but they all seem to know one another and are making morning office small talk. Just another day at work for them, while I sit with butterflies dancing a polka in my stomach.

By eleven the judge has still not arrived.

I thought the driver who hit me and his horrible wife who accused me of faking would show up. I was so looking forward to them hearing every gruesome detail of the Disneyland that is my life now, but I guess they have more important things to do. They'll probably just make a drop-in appearance to testify. I wonder if they'll try telling the jury that I jumped on their car and elbowed their windshield out, like they told the police officer at the scene of the accident? That should get a laugh out of the jury because it definitely got one out of the cop.

The church-pew wooden bench is wreaking havoc on my lower back, and it's not doing wonders for my bony butt, either. The judge's empty chair looks to be a lot more comfortable than the torture device that we are forced to sit on. I ponder whether this is intentional.

Still no judge. It's noon and time to break for lunch.

I exit the courtroom and begin to shuffle down the hallway. I can feel the jurors' eyes following me as they collect their belongings for the break. I am sure they are not pleased with the fact that they have been stuck sitting in the hallway for two hours after having the trial postponed for two weeks. I can only imagine how this entire process has disrupted their lives, and I pray that they will not blame me for their inconvenience.

My mother and I sit across from each other at a dive diner in catatonic states. She forces me to order a salad, but no matter how much I drown it in dressing it still tastes as limp and lifeless as I feel. My nerves are stretched to the point of breaking. Everything seems surreal, and although I know I am awake, I can't help but feel that I am dreaming, because the whole day is too weird and awful to be real. I begin to fear the judge will never arrive and my case will never be heard.

We head back to the courtroom, and by two p.m., there's still no judge. My mother and Legal Eagle and I are all staring off into space, and the male rumpled-suit lawyer is telling the female lawyer in the too-tight suit a story just loud enough for the entire room to hear. It's a funny little story about getting into a fight with his ex-wife and trashing his apartment and breaking random pieces of furniture. I am making a mental note never to marry a lawyer and wondering where the fuck Judge Lush has been for the past four hours. I'm going to have to guess that she's sharpening her pitchfork in hell. The three employees of the court have now taken to reading their individual papers, and as they turn each page, it grates on my fragile nerves a little more. I feel like a character in *Waiting for Godot*, which is a great play, but I have no desire to actually live through it. It's a subject of debate among scholars whether Godot represented God or was merely a derivative of the French slang word for "boot," and I think now I have finally unraveled the mystery. My Godot is both a God and a boot, or at least she thinks she is a God, and she's shoving her boot up my injured ass every hour that she makes us wait.

The rumpled-suit lawyer has finished his tale of marital bliss and the air is now thick with silence. Legal Eagle, my mother, and I share glances of despair. It is now after two thirty, and the legal aide, a strapping young man who looks like he could have played

college football, has walked into the courtroom and is holding
the door open, and like a vision of debauchery and injustice, Judge
Lush makes her entrance, sashaying into the courtroom as if
she hasn't a care in the world. Her locks are coiffed in a Suzanne
Somers side ponytail, and her cat-eye glasses are low on her nose,
as she peers over them to wave in an oddly flirtatious way to her
captive audience.

"Hello, counselors, so nice to see you," she says to the opposing
legal team. To Legal Eagle she says, "Hello, counselor, so glad you
could join us today." Her strange Southern drawl strikes me as
obviously fake. She's like Blanche DuLaw. She proceeds to ascend
her judge's throne and call one of her friends on the phone to
make idle chitchat about being at a funeral this morning while we
all watch on in horror. Another funeral? Is she killing people in
her spare time? Because she is certainly killing me.

My mother leans over and whispers in my ear, "My poor baby,
you are so fucked."

My lawyer taps me on the shoulder and gestures for me to follow him out into the hallway. I trail behind him and take a seat in
the empty corridor where the jury used to be. Legal Eagle is pacing in front of me. "I have never seen anything like this. She has
no intention of trying your case. You lost twenty-seven-thousand
dollars today in doctors' testimonies, and she'll show up late tomorrow, too, and you'll lose another twenty-seven thousand."

"How is this legal? What should I do?" I am looking into Legal
Eagle's eyes for an answer, and I see a man who believed in something once.

The strapping young legal aide comes out into the hallway.
"Have you come to a decision on the settlement?" he forcibly asks
Legal Eagle.

"No, we haven't, and we know exactly what's going on here," Legal Eagle snaps back. The legal aide goes back into the court-room, and Legal Eagle takes a seat next to me on the bench. "I'm afraid if you try this case with her you'll get nothing."

I sit in the courtroom hallway, staring at the floor and weigh-ing my options, which are bleak. Try a case with a crazy woman and possibly get nothing, or settle and at least be able to cover my outstanding medical bills and doctors' testimonies, and pay back the loan sharks. It won't cover a lifetime of the future medical bills that I will have to pay out of pocket, since I am now one big pre-existing condition. It won't give me back the past two years, and it won't give me back my health, but she has left me no choice. I can't request a new judge. It's her or nothing. I know what I have to do.

Legal Eagle is just as crestfallen as I am as we walk back into the courtroom. The jury is ushered in, taking their individual seats in the box, and for the first time, I really look at them, and in that instant I know that they would have given me a fair trial, but the judge has made sure that they will never know my story, never know the pain and the trauma I have faced, and never have the opportunity to rule in my favor.

"Well, it seems like we've reached a settlement. I would like to thank the jury for your time. I'm sure you have places to be, so you're free to go now. Bye-bye," she says in her bogus Blanche DuLaw drawl.

The jury turns to look at me with pity-filled gazes, and I try desperately not to cry. My mother, on the other hand, is not doing very well at masking her despair.

We walk back to Legal Eagle's office in silence. I don't know how to express what I am feeling. I don't believe in anything any-

more. It's all a big façade: the health care system, the welfare system, the legal system . . . nobody cares about righting injustice or
caring for their fellow man.

"Sweetheart, aren't you coming up?"

"I'll be up in a second, Mom. I'm just going to smoke a cigarette. I like a good cigarette after I get screwed."

I walk across the street from Legal Eagle's office and light up.
Yeah, I don't really need to add cancer to my list of problems, but
I am clinging to the wreckage and marveling over the fact that I
couldn't even get a speaking part in my own fucking trial. I glance
down and notice where I am standing. I am right by the pit where
the twin towers used to stand. It reminds me that after 9/11, for
at least a couple of weeks, we weren't different races or social
classes; we were one and concerned for one another's well-being.
Cheering on firefighters, donating blood, packing up water and
food for the workers. Why did it take something as huge and as
tragic as that for us to care about our neighbors? And why did it
stop?

We tend as a society to dissociate ourselves from problems that
don't directly affect our lives, until they touch us or our family
and friends. If someone had told me three years ago that I was
going to get hit by a car, live in constant pain, end up on welfare,
and lose friends and all my money, I would have told him that
he was crazy. That could never happen to me. You know, I think
in a moment of perspective, maybe this accident was the change I
needed . . . just not the change I wanted. Maybe I needed to know
what happens to people who don't have medical insurance in this
country. Maybe I needed to know that even people who have insurance aren't getting the care they deserve. That families living
below the poverty line are only allowed to eat about four dollars

and seventy-something cents of food a day. Maybe I needed to actually experience it, instead of just reading a statistic in a paper or hearing a story on the news, to remember that we are all in this together and that we all need a little help sometimes.

I'm a little surprised at myself for being so philosophical after getting so royally screwed, but there it is. This chapter of my life is over . . . good, bad, or indifferent, my season in hell is done. For two years the thought of justice being served at my trial was my light at the end of the tunnel, and now it's gone. I need to pick up the pieces and create a new light and a new tunnel, and in some far-off tomorrow, I will get better. I will be happy and healthy again. Tonight, however, I will go home and scream into a pillow every swear word in the book while picturing Judge Lush's unjust face and her hideous Suzanne Somers side ponytail.

CHAPTER TWELVE

Gandhi Land Diaries

Dear Diary,

It has been a year since the trial that never was. A year filled with small personal achievements and growth . . . God, that makes me sound like one of those inspirational quote-a-day calendars.

With my memory finally improving, I felt confident enough to start auditioning again, and I booked the first job I went up for, which, ironically enough, was a car commercial. My head wasn't anywhere near the windshield, though. The spot thankfully ran a lot on TV, making me eligible for SAG (Screen Actors Guild) health insurance, and they don't discriminate against people with preexisting conditions. I need to make about fifteen thousand dollars annually from acting to qualify for the health insurance, which will cover me for a year. So that is one major hurdle that I got over, since no other health care providers will touch my preexisting butt with a ten-foot pole.

This year has been an uphill struggle toward recovery, and I have been tackling it like an athlete trains for competition—only my competition is my body and the prize is to one day be pain-free. I go to the gym five days a week and do physical therapy exercising, which involves me in suggestive poses with a rather large plastic ball. My mom calls them my porno exercises because I look like I am humping the ball rather than strengthening my back; it has, however, made me popular with the gym rats. I also do Pilates once a week on a reformer, which resembles a device of torture; despite the intimidating design, it was created to help strengthen injured people's core muscles in prison camps during World War I.

Since I don't want any more epidurals shoved up my tailbone, and I am morally opposed to having my spine carved on by a surgeon until they figure out that whole stem-cell situation, I have turned to a more Eastern approach to medicine to alleviate my persistent back injuries. I started with acupuncture, which helped for short periods of time, but by the next day the pain would be back. So my acupuncturist referred me to a nonaggressive chiropractor. No cracking or jarring of the spine; this doctor focuses on alignment, symmetry, and kinesiology. She reads my body like a map, and can tell just by touching me which part of my back is acting up on that particular day. It's kind of fascinating how the human body works; I can be having excruciating pain in my lower back, and she will discover that it's actually coming from my neck, and vice versa. It barely feels like she's touching me at all; it's like the lightest most delicate massage, which helps strengthen weak muscles, restore balance, and improve mobility. I'm kind of her pet project because she's never seen someone with such a messed-up spinal column, and she is determined to "unravel my spine." This seems to be the only thing that has helped me in the past three years, and sometimes I go a whole two days without pain, which might not sound like much to the average person, but after three years of nonstop, unrelenting agony, it's like a two-day trip to Disneyland for me.

Speaking of trips—I am taking one. Since I have been aggressively pursuing my physical recovery, it is time to start healing my mind from all the emotional trauma that I have been through. I think that after a traumatic event, the brain compartmentalizes things so that you can deal with them in the moment and get through it, but then you need to step back and really absorb everything that has happened so that you can move on. I haven't been able to do that yet. I haven't been able to let go of the trauma, the anger, or the fear. I think a doctor would probably call it post-traumatic stress disorder, but my mother would say I need to pull my head out of my ass.

I got it in my mind about six months ago that the place I need to go to do this mental healing is India. I had no idea how I was going to make it happen, but I started telling anyone who would listen that this was my plan, and then two months ago I told the right person. My brother's best friend has a round-trip, first-class ticket to India that he has to use by the end of the year, and when he heard that I was hoping to go, he just gave me his ticket. So I am leaving tomorrow to travel to India by myself for two months. I have no set plans after the first two weeks. I will be staying in Mumbai for three days, or at least I think I will. I called to make a hotel reservation, and the man hung up on me twice. So I guess I won't know until I get there if a car will be picking me up at the airport to take me to my reserved hotel room, or if I'll be hanging out on the side of the road with a holy cow. After Mumbai, I will head to a ten-day silent Vipassana meditation retreat, in the hope that it will not only help me heal my mind but also help me manage my pain better. I'm not sure how I am going to shut up for ten days, but we'll cross that silent bridge when we get to it. And then I will see where India takes me. No agendas, no doctors, no government offices, no reminders . . . just me. I am excited and nervous, but I think I have all bases covered, thanks to Bud, who made me buy out the sporting goods store. I'm sure I won't use any of it, but I am so prepared I could probably go camping in the Amazon for six months. It's all packed in my Swiss Army backpack (which thankfully has wheels), along with two pairs of pants and four shirts . . . when one has to carry her own bag half-way across the world, there's no room for fashion. Did I really just say that? Maybe my brain injury isn't as healed as I thought. I kid; I'm just leaving room to buy some cute Indian outfits because one must always be appropriately dressed.

So, this is it . . . this is my journal, or as I am calling it, my Gandhi Land Diaries. I will chart my progress, adventures, and probably some misadventures, on my journey of healing. Well, that's all for now, I better get to sleep; I've got an early flight tomorrow . . . can you say "first class"?

P.S. Almost forgot. I ran into Aura (Little Miss "Ask the Universe for a Change"), and when I told her I was going to

India, she suggested that I find a guru when I'm over there. I assured her that I would not be looking for a guru. I'll be looking at the sights. I'm not taking any more advice from that girl.

. . . .

Dear Diary,

The journey from New York to London was a breeze. I must say, Virgin first-class has spoiled me forever. All the chairs fold out into beds, with fluffy down comforters, and I had my own TV with all newly released films. It's like a fancy flying hotel, and the food is actually edible and quite tasty, with a bottomless glass of wine, if you so desire . . . and I desired. Oh, and I almost forgot the complimentary manicures and massages. For the first two hours of the flight I kept getting this overwhelming sense that they were going to kick me back to coach for being an imposter. I was reluctant to ask for anything; I tried to unfold my bed by myself, which I guess is a no-no; first-class people don't do for themselves. And when they walked around taking reservations for manicures and massages, I politely declined, even though I was dying for one. I was feeling guilty: I was on food stamps a year ago; I don't deserve to be flying across the world in the lap of luxury. I guess if you kick a dog enough, it starts to feel that it deserves it; so after a glass of wine, I had to pet my inner Lassie and remind myself that I do deserve the good things in life. I decided to test this out by asking the flight attendant for another glass of wine, and she gave me the whole bottle. Yeah, it's like magic, this attitude stuff. I think with a little practice and a little more liquid courage, I might actually start believing it, and until then, I'm going to fake it until I make it.

I'm sitting in the Virgin lounge in the UK right now, waiting for my connecting flight to Delhi. There is something about the transient nature of airports that I just love. Everybody is either going somewhere or coming home from somewhere. They either have stories of their journeys or are looking forward to having stories. Speaking of stories, nobody knows mine; I am anonymous out here. Nobody knows about the accident, nobody knows that I was a welfare queen, nobody knows how truly dark my life got. I was just speaking to a woman who is on her way home to Nairobi. She asked me if I was going to India to find myself. I told her I wasn't, because I hate that cliché, but the truth is I think that's exactly what I'm hoping to find in India. I think I somehow lost myself over the past three years, and I am looking forward to meeting the woman I have become.

Well, they just called my flight; gotta go like a first-class ho. I'll write more when I touch down in Gandhi Land.

. . . .

Namaste Diary,

On the flight from London to Delhi, I sat across from a rather distinguished looking man in his fifties. I became fascinated watching him as I pretended to read. He had a book placed in his lap, and he would turn the pages with his left hand as his right hand stayed stationary by his side. When the meal came, his wife, who was sitting next to me, moved over to sit next to him, took his book, and then meticulously cut up his chicken for him. I could see the irritation and resentment growing in his eyes as she lovingly did this, and the frustrated look on his face as he tried to maneuver the fork with his left hand. When he got cream sauce on his lip, he snapped at his wife when she went to hand him a napkin. She did not argue or fight, she simply placed it back down next to his plate and moved back to her seat next to me and continued to watch, lovingly, from across the aisle.

After the meal, he drifted off to sleep, and his wife, a very lovely English woman, began to talk to me. I could tell she needed someone to listen. Her husband was a very prominent heart surgeon, and a year ago he'd had a stroke, which affected the right side of his body. She told me how frustrating it is for him. This once vibrant man's entire life changed in a split second, and now he is a prisoner of a body that doesn't work the way it used to. They are traveling to India for six months for him to be treated by a doctor who has revolutionary treatments and therapies for stroke victims that haven't made it to London or the States yet because of the FDA (and the equivalent in the UK). She pointed out that she didn't know what they would have done if they didn't have the money to afford the best health care the world has to offer. I could have told her exactly what would have happened if they didn't have money, but she did not need to hear it.

I did find it fascinating that India has superior, cutting-edge medical techniques that haven't yet made it to the

United States and England, which are considered two of the most powerful countries in the world.

Anyway, if love can heal, this woman is sure to get her husband better. It was inspiring to see how much she loved him, and he loved her, too; he's just frustrated that this happened to him and frustrated with his body . . . and boy do I know how that goes.

Arriving in Delhi, I was reluctant to say good-bye to my first-class accommodations because I am quite positive that this is as fancy as my trip is going to get . . . I'm a girl on a budget, after all. It wasn't until I exited the plane to look for my connecting domestic flight to Mumbai that I was informed that the domestic and international airports were a half hour cab ride apart, which was going to make catching my connecting flight tricky but not impossible. I claimed my luggage and went out to the cab stand, which was a wooden plank held up by two metal barrels. The man behind the makeshift desk asked me where I was going and then handed me a card with the price and the number of my cab. There were about fifty cars, all parked on top of one another, so I walked around having a "Holy shit, Toto, we're not in Kansas anymore" moment, looking for the matching number. My cab was a beat-up VW-type minibus with no windows, and my driver was about twelve. I crammed into the backseat with my head grazing the roof, and the driver started the car . . . only it wouldn't start, it kept stalling. This went on for five minutes until I finally said, "Should I get another cab, because I'm going to miss my flight?" At which point my twelve-year-old chauffer got out of the car, pulled out the driver's seat, hotwired the car, shoved the seat back in, and off we went. Driving in India is like nothing I have ever seen before; they drive like maniacs, cutting each other off, and pedestrians walk right across the freeway, as if they are immune to getting hit. And the cows do the same, knowing no one would dare hit them—citizens can actually be sent to jail for killing or harming the sacred animal. Then there are the motorbikes. I didn't know it was possible for a family of five to ride on one motorcycle, but it is. I was sure that not only was I going to miss my flight but also I was going to die. Which would be ironic, considering what I've been through, and it would put a damper on seeing the sights and my journal entries. But I didn't die. I made my flight (barely), and I told my driver that he could definitely have a future in Nascar once he can see over the steering wheel.

Arriving in Mumbai, I wasn't sure if I'd have a car meeting me, let alone a hotel reservation. But much to my amazement, in the sea of people, I spotted a sign with my name on it . . . well, kind of—my name was spelled Hedan Borgman— but it was close enough. When I got to the hotel they showed me to my room, which I have since lovingly named the Crack Shack, or the Utility Closet. It was on the first floor near the front desk. A room no bigger than a closet, with no windows. The bathroom was one big shower with a drain in the middle of the floor, and contained a small toilet with a hose next to it and a bucket of "ass water" . . . Yep, they're not really a toilet paper culture. I was too exhausted to have a heart attack, but I did ask if all the rooms were the same, and the concierge told me I could move rooms the next day. My new room would be considered a Holiday Inn–type room, but after a night in the Crack Shack, it looks like the Plaza to me.

It has a real shower and bathtub, windows, and, more important, no bucket of ass water.

This morning I met some Russian backpackers at breakfast, drinking vodka in their coffee. They told me it helped
prevent "Delhi Belly" and offered me some. Although dysen-
tery doesn't sound appealing, or fun, I decided to take my
chances and pass on the Bukowski breakfast; I have a strict
seven p.m. rule when it comes to drinking.

Well, off to explore Mumbai . . . more exciting entries to
come.

. . . .

Dear Diary,

I have recovered from jet lag and am still working on the
culture shock. The poverty here is overwhelming. People
sleeping on the street, children following me for blocks begging for money, crippled beggars that are maimed by their
parents as infants to bring in more money. It is heartbreaking
to bear witness to the destitute conditions that so many call
their daily lives. The children are especially gut wrenching.
No child should ever have to go hungry or be without shelter.
They are all so beautiful, and you can see the desperation in
their young eyes. There are no such things as food stamps
here, no helping hand to give the poor a shot at a better life
or food in their stomachs. When I was on food stamps, I received four dollars and seventy-something cents a day; it is
hard to nourish yourself on that in the States, but here it

would really help. Each day that I am in India, I make sure to give a child the four dollars and seventy cents; it doesn't really feel like enough, but maybe it is a helping hand like the one that was given to me. I also have restaurants pack up any food that I don't finish, and I give it to someone begging. Nothing should go to waste in a country with so many hungry. I really wish I could help all of them, but I can only help one or two a day. To tell the truth, they are probably helping me more than I'm helping them. I thought I knew poverty, but this is a whole different level. I think I identify more with the beggars than I do with the tourists. I was walking behind a couple today dressed in their wannabe Indian garb, with their California kumbaya pretense showing through. The man said, "Whatever you do, don't give the beggars money; you'll only encourage them." The woman smiled and nodded. "There won't be any beggars at the ashram, will there?" she questioned. I wanted to punch them in the face. They come here and they dress more Indian than the Indians and they'll go to their fancy ashram trying to buy back their souls as they block out and avoid what India is. It is just as ugly as it is beautiful, just as cruel as it is kind . . . but they will never see the India that I am seeing, and hope to see yet. They will go back to the States with saris and linen, telling all those who will listen how enlightened they are, and only I will know that the five-year-old girl that they didn't want to encourage as they walked by on their road to Nirvana now has food to put in her stomach, thanks to me.

I was warned about First World guilt, but I think it's more survivor's guilt for me. Listening to those people, I was reminded of the cashier in the grocery store telling me to put the groceries back on the shelves when my food stamp card was declined. I could hear the woman at the food stamp office saying to me that all of our stories sound the same, right before she threw me out of the office and refused to help me. All the condescending voices of cruelty echoed in my head back to a time when I was the one in need. As I looked at the little girl, I saw myself in her: hungry, alone, and desperately in need of kindness. India is like a mirror that is forcing me to put things in perspective and remove the masks and labels that defined me for the past three years, but I don't think I will ever forget how it feels to be hungry.

In stark contrast to the poverty, the architecture is beautiful here and bursting with vibrant colors. I have been attacking the city, not wanting to miss a single thing. I have seen the Temple Caves on Elephant Island, the hanging gardens, Gandhi's house, the Dhobi Ghat, the gateway to India, and a Jain temple. At the Jain temple my tour guide asked me if I had my period, at which point I answered, "Yeah, I do. Why, do you need a tampon?" I read that in India tampons are slightly contraband. She laughed and said, "No, but you can't go in the temple if you have your period. The Jains consider women to be unholy during that time of the month." That injured every bone in my feminist body, but it's their place and their rules, so my unholy self could only take pictures from the outside. I have been taking pictures like crazy. I don't want to forget a single moment or a single beautiful face. The children love to see their digital images, and I love to see them smile. Even with the hardships of their daily lives, they still smile, and that is one lesson I have learned from them.

I am off to my Vipassana meditation retreat tomorrow, so I won't be writing any journal entries for the next ten days, but I'm sure I'll have plenty to say and write when I am done. For instance, a guide to how to carry on a conversation with yourself in your head for ten days. What to do when you have to scratch your nose for three hours but you can't move. And bitchy narcissistic temper tantrums in silence.

Those who are about to die salute you.

. . . .

Dear Diary,

I should really rethink my career in the States and just move to India. During my three days in Mumbai I was stopped five times and asked to be in a Bollywood film, and when I arrived at the Vipassana meditation retreat, two teenage girls asked me if I was Cameron Diaz. I guess all of us blond chicks look the same. I told them I was Cameron's meditation stunt double, because she was too busy helping Justin bring his sexy back to get her Dhamma on.

All my friends were betting as to how long I would last at the retreat. I think the general consensus was three days, although my mom was putting her money on two days. Oh, ye of little faith. Well, I made it all ten days; no talking, no music, no reading, no writing, just me meditating.

I arrived at the retreat at eleven a.m. for check-in, which took a while, being that there were about four hundred people. I was one of two Americans, and there were twenty

Europeans—everybody else was Indian. Since the retreat is donation only and not for profit, you have the poorest of the poor with the richest of the rich, all coming together to the one place in this country where they are equals. They eat the same food, sleep in the same accommodations, follow the same rules, and acquire the same peace of mind that meditation hopefully will give them. There are also no dogmas or -isms allowed here. If you pray to the east, kneel at a cross, or perform any other form of worship, you must put it on hold for the ten days and only practice Vipassana (which means "to see things as they really are") meditation and Dhamma (which is just basically being a good and mindful person). So there are no pissing contests about whose God is better. (My hypothesis is that we are all God, and it is our own personal journey that someday will lead us all to realizing happiness, giving up hardship and strife, and acknowledging that we are all the same. Many would disagree with me, but just as I respect their philosophies and beliefs, I hope they respect mine, because at the end of the day, none of us know for sure what this big, crazy trip called life is all about.) So I was fine with the no praying, but I'm sure it was hard for a lot of people, since India is a country that is deeply immersed in religion, as well as divided by it. It was inspiring to see Buddhists, Hindus, Muslims, Christians, Jews, and nonbelievers all coming together on common ground to have their own deeply personal experiences while sharing in the learning of this particular type of meditation.

The center, called Dhamma Guri, is nestled in between the mountains in Igatpuri, which is three hours outside of Mumbai. It is a magical setting, surrounded by rust-colored mountains and green foliage that is so vibrant that it almost looks fake. The nature is complemented by the structure of the buildings and the use of soothing whites and rich golds. I was surprised at how nice the facilities were. I even had my own private room. There was, however, a bucket of ass water in the bathroom, but the ass water and I have become sort of friends now . . . not close friends, mind you, more like distant acquaintances that treat each other with polite reserve. After I got settled into my room, we had a meal and enjoyed the last few minutes of talking that we would have for the next ten days. I chatted with an Australian woman who had done the course before, trying to pump her for information because I was starting to get nervous. All she said was, "This will be the hardest thing you ever do in your life but the most rewarding." Yeah, that didn't do much to quell my fears, especially since it was moments before we took the vow of silence and got the strict schedule.

4 a.m. Wake up

4:30 a.m.–6:30 a.m. Meditate

6:30 a.m.–7:00 a.m. Breakfast

7:00 a.m.–8:00 a.m. Shower, because it's the only time there is hot water

8:00 a.m.–11:00 a.m. Meditate

11:00 a.m. Lunch, which is your last meal of the day

1:00 p.m. Meditate

2:00 p.m. Meditate

3:00 p.m. Meditate

4:00 p.m. Meditate

5:00 p.m. Tea break

6:00 p.m. Meditate

7:00 p.m. Meditate

7:30 p.m. Video discourse on the practice of
　　Vipassana and Dhamma

And just when you think you can't meditate anymore . . .
guess what, you can.

9:00 p.m. Go to bed

9:30 p.m. Lights out

Now I haven't gone to bed at nine thirty since I was eight years old, but then again, I have never gotten up at four a.m. except for sex. And after countless hours of meditating, my ass was so one with my meditation cushion that I still thought I was sitting when I was lying down in my bed.

The woman in the room next to mine was having a hard time with the silence and would shout things in her sleep, like, "You're not getting the fucking point. The purple people will be kings." These midnight outbursts startled me at first, but then I began to look forward to them. They kind of broke up the deafening silence.

Most people's idea of meditation is that it is navel gazing. That you just sit with your eyes closed and do nothing, but let me tell you, this meditation is hard work. It's like coal mining of the mind. And after the past three years, I had a lot of mining to do.

For the first three and a half days we practiced Anapana meditation, where you focus your attention on your breath, which helps you develop control over your ornery mind. But this was harder than expected. The first three days I was silently full of anger. I hated the woman who directed us into the meditation hall as if we were cattle. I despised the woman who sat across from me at every meal, who refused to use silverware, shoving the food in her mouth like a two-year-old. I was agitated by the person who would meditate during the tea break, as if proving to us that we were nothing in the wake of her Buddha-like self. I loathed the woman next to me in the meditation hall who would let out these monstrous burps. I counted ten burps in one hour. I kept thinking, what the hell? She's eating the same food as I am; where are these burps coming from? Somebody give this bitch a Tums because she is messing up my meditation. But what I really hated was that I was thinking all these horrible thoughts. I am not generally an angry person, and I didn't know where all this anger and rage were coming from. I hated feeling this way, and I wanted to run away from this place and from myself. And if I were somewhere else and not in the middle of nowhere in India, I probably would have.

Halfway through the third day we started practicing Vipassana meditation, where you scan your body for sensations, systematically moving from your head to your toes. You must not linger on any body part too long. If my lower back was hurting, or my knee was killing me, I couldn't focus on it, I had to move on to the next body part. It teaches you not to get attached. There is no pain, there is no pleasure, there are just sensations. This was a hard concept for me to grasp at first, because I was thinking, don't tell me there's no pain—I got hit by a fucking car. But maybe that's the problem; maybe I had become attached to the story just as much as I had become attached to the pain.

By the fourth day I had resigned myself to the fact that I would stick it out. I started getting more immersed in my meditation, and the outside annoyances started to drift away. But then I was inside my head, surrounded by all the shit I had pushed down over the years. The anger, the pain, the humiliation, the fear, and the guilt all came flooding back to me in Technicolor. I could see it, touch it, taste it, smell it, and hear it, in sensory overload, and I couldn't use any of my usual coping mechanisms (like a big fat glass of wine, or listening to music) to avoid it. I just had to sit there and observe it as it played out on the flat-screen TV in my head. Practitioners say this type of meditation is like performing surgery on your mind, but what they don't point out is that it is without the benefit of anesthesia. You have to face yourself head-on, and my emotions hit me with as much force as the car that caused all my problems. I realized that in order to let go of the anger and all the other negative feelings swirling inside me, I had to find a way to forgive: forgive myself. It makes no sense, but I was still carrying around this unbelievable guilt that maybe in some way I asked for this to happen to me by asking the universe for a change, by not having health insurance; and I needed to forgive myself for everything that had happened. Then I had to forgive the man who hit me. I had to forgive the woman that yelled, "Stand up! You're not hurt! I'm a doctor—I know you're not hurt!" (I won't lie that the word *cunt* didn't keep popping up in my head for quite a while, but eventually it went away.) I had to forgive the government workers that were mean to me. I had to forgive the friends that walked away from me, I had to forgive the judge . . . and so on, and so on.

I had to let it all go. I couldn't be attached to it anymore because it would ultimately eat me like a cancer, and I don't want to be one of those miserable bitter people who let one moment in time define who they are and set the tragic tone for the rest of their lives. I want to be happy. Yeah, this horrible thing happened to me, but horrible things happen to people every day. I want to be one of the ones who takes a negative and turns it into a positive.

I meditated on this for a few days, trying to figure out how I could make the lemons that life had given me into lemon margaritas. It's amazing how clarity comes to you when you clean all the bullshit out of your head, and I think I've figured out how to turn it all around. The two things that make me the happiest in life are acting and helping people. With acting I am usually telling other people's stories, but now I've got my own story. I've never really written anything before, but I've lived this, so I'm pretty sure I can write it. I think it should be a one-woman show. I mean, actresses are always bitching that there aren't enough good roles for women, so I'll just write about twenty-five roles for me, 'cause why the fuck not. But more important, I will be telling a story that will echo the stories of millions of Americans who slip through the cracks of our failed health care and welfare systems everyday. This will be their show, just as much as it will be mine. And maybe the audience will walk away knowing that if something like this can happen to a five-foot-ten-inch, white ex-model, it could happen to them, too. None of us is immune.

I practically levitated off the meditation cushion that was firmly glued to my ass when this epiphany came to me. I'm not sure how I'm going to make it happen yet, but just like I wasn't sure how I was going to survive those two years, and I wasn't sure how I was going to get here to India, I'll figure it out.

My mental surgery has been a success. I have faced my demons and let them go; I have learned to observe my physical pain instead of drowning in it; I have come to the conclusion that if I shut the hell up for copious amounts of time, I will find that I already have all the answers I need. Meditation will be a tool to help me live a more equanimous existence.

That Australian woman was right on the money.

And today, when I walked out of the retreat, I was happy, like a child on Christmas morning who has received the best present of all: I have my life back, and it's all shiny and new . . . or maybe this is the first day of my life and I was born right here in India.

So . . . om shanti that.

Next stop: the holy city of Varanasi to confront my fear of death.

. . . .

Dear Diary,

There are things worse than a twenty-four-hour train ride in India, but I have to say that it probably runs a close second to a colonoscopy. I had this idea that the train would be packed with tourists and backpackers engaging me in good conversations to pass the time. Wrong. My sleeper car was populated with Indian men who proceeded to stare at me for the first six hours of the journey, until most of them finally fell asleep. I, however, was not lucky enough to pass out, and not for lack of trying. Anytime I would start to drift off, a man would open the drawn curtains around my bottom bunk, look at me for a few seconds, and then close them. I felt like the sideshow act at the circus . . . look at the blond freak. I also made the mistake of trying to use the bathroom. As if squat toilets aren't hard enough to use, it is impossible on a moving train. I'm not proud of it, but I have peed on my own foot five times since I've been in India, and we can now rack it up to an even six. All in all, the trip was the most unusual way I've spent Christmas, but it did keep the usual holiday family drama to a minimum. However, eating a bag of cashews for dinner instead of the typical Christmas fare was a little unsatisfying. But it was all worth it (all twenty-four long hours) because Varanasi is the most mystical place I have ever seen. Legend has it that the city was founded by Lord Shiva. It is the oldest city in India, at about three thousand years, and it looks every bit its age, in an old-world antique way. It is located on the banks of the River Ganges, which is supposed to have the power of washing away one's sins. Hindus believe that those who die and are cremated here are liberated from the cycle of reincarnation and suffering.

I've thought a lot about death over the past three years. According to the statistics, the EMT, and the police officer, the accident should have killed me. I've been confronted with the truth of my mortality, and the fact that I *should* have died, and didn't, scares me just as much as death itself. I miraculously escaped death, but during the worst times that followed I sometimes longed for it, as if I were flaunting my own existence.

Here in Varanasi, death is a constant companion. I pass men in the labyrinth of tiny alleyways carrying corpses on stretchers. I watch the bodies burn on the funeral pyres down on the ghants. I see the ashes float by in the water. But here death is celebrated rather than mourned. Every evening there is a ceremony down by the river, with chanting and music and candles that light up the sky. And every morning at sunrise I watch people bathing and performing their morning prayers in the river. I find it a little frightening that they bathe, wash their clothes, and sometimes drink the water of a river that contains human ashes. Faith is indeed a powerful force—and they must have rocking immune systems. I did toy with the idea of getting in the water, until I saw a half-burned corpse float by. Although I am getting more comfortable with death and dying, I don't really want to do the backstroke with it.

Walking around yesterday, I met three adorable ten-year-old boys who decided to appoint themselves my personal tour guides through the maze of alleyways that make up Varanasi. We drank chai standing on a street corner watching cows stroll by. They took me to the Golden Temple, and then they asked me if I knew Goldie Hawn. It seems that Goldie has been coming to Varanasi for years and always shops in one of the boy's uncle's stores. So, of course, now I was en route to the uncle's because that's how things work in India.

I walked into the shop, and it was a shrine to Goldie Hawn. There were pictures and letters hanging on the walls, and I was subjected to looking at two photo albums. I can honestly say that no one has seen this much Goldie since the eighties. Papo, the owner, was a jovial fellow, with a face that was one big smile and a laugh that made his whole body shake. My three adorable boys made their commission. I got two beautiful silk scarves, the pleasure of Papo's company, and enough Goldie to last me a lifetime. After I got Gold-iefied, I decided to go to an STD and email Bud and Mary Jane. I still find it amusing that the place where you can use computers or telephones has the same initials as sexually transmitted diseases, but English *is* their second language. Anyway, I wanted to email Bud because before I left for India, he made me buy all this stuff that I was sure I was never going to use: a high-tech water purifier, a travel sheet, a first-aid kit, a flashlight, hydrating salts, three padlocks, ugly hiking san-dals, three types of mosquito repellants, and a Leatherman (it's like a Swiss Army knife). Quite frankly, I bought it just to shut him up. He quit smoking pot because Mary Jane is pregnant, and you don't argue with a man who is desperately missing his Jamaican herbs and living with a crazy pregnant woman.

Well, move aside J.C., Buddha, and Allah, there is a new god in town, and his name is Bud. I sleep in the travel sheet every night. The flashlight is a lifesaver during the random blackouts that happen in India. I am so one with my ugly hiking sandals that I could possibly wear them forever. My perfume of choice is ode de mosquito repellant. I have used my padlocks to lock my backpack, my hotel door, and my chastity belt. My Leatherman has come in handy for fixing things, and just having it gives me a false sense of security with my fan club of Indian men. And, last but not least, my fancy water purifier is the envy of every sick tourist I meet, and I'm thinking of charging people ten rupees to admire it.

They emailed me back today. Bud is pleased that I am using all of the gadgets, and Mary Jane gave birth to a healthy baby girl. She named her Lula May, which is the real name of Holly Golightly in *Breakfast at Tiffany's*. I think it's kind of a testament to our friendship, since the first day we met we watched the movie three times in a row. I guess the palm reader we encountered in Paris all those years ago was right. Mary Jane would meet her soul mate, this relationship would last forever, and they would have three children. And something would happen to me, where I should die but I don't. It would be a miracle that I live, and it would change my life forever. It would be a rebirth, and a gift. And as I leave the city of death, after confronting my fear, it is comforting to know that the circle of life continues and that I have a new little person to look forward to meeting when I get home.

. . . .

Dear Diary,

Since I have been in India, I have seen palaces, temples, and mosques. I have walked barefoot through the rat temple (home to some twenty thousand rats, and yes, a few scampered across my feet), rode a camel named Michael Jackson through the desert of Rajasthan (which was probably not the smartest thing for a person with a back injury to do), and shared my breakfast with a monkey (who could outeat Kirstie Alley). But I still had one thing more to do before leaving India. My mother told me before I left not to bother coming back to the States unless I had a picture of myself on the bench in front of the Taj Mahal, like the famous picture of Princess Diana. I had no idea what she was talking about, but I told her I'd get it done. She even went so far as to tell me what Diana was wearing, saying that it would be really nice if I wore an outfit like she had on. At that point, I said, "Easy, demanding. I'll get you the picture, but I'm not making any promises about the wardrobe."

So at six a.m. this morning, I arrived at the Taj. I was one of about twenty other fools that got up at this ungodly hour, and I was freezing my tits off in my shirt and skirt. No, I wasn't dressed like Diana; I do have my boundaries. Sorry, Mom. I hired a photographer to take my mother's pictures. Twelve pictures for twenty-five dollars, which is highway robbery in India. I told him I would meet him back at the infamous bench once the sun came up and in the meantime I would check out the Taj with a guide. The guide's English was marginal at best, and he insisted on talking really fast, which made him completely unintelligible and just made me laugh, which made him angry. When I told him that I couldn't understand him, he insisted that he spoke perfect English and had learned it from watching an American show called *Baywatch*. I didn't really care because the Taj is one of the most astoundingly beautiful buildings I have ever seen, and when staring at absolute perfection I find it best to laugh. Little did I know that my Pamela Anderson tour was just a warmup for my cheesy Taj photographer. We met at said bench . . . me still freezing my tits off and him comfy and warmed by the money that he was taking from me.

"Come over here near the tree . . . put this flower in your hair and look up at the Taj," he instructed.

"Okay, listen, Avedon, there will be no flowers, no longing looks at the Taj. I just need a picture on the bench."

"Oh, Princess Diana," he replied with the customary head bobble.

"Holy shit. Did my mom call you, too? Yes, Princess Diana, that's what I want."

Suddenly, we spoke the same language. He did take twenty pictures instead of twelve and tried to sell me the extra eight photos, but I declined. Twelve will be more than enough pictures for my mom to make wallpaper and get me back in the country.

Making my way to my next destination, and I'm sure looking completely lost, I stopped a middle-aged Indian man to ask for directions, and he offered to show me the way. His crisp linen suit glistened in the early morning sun as we walked for a while in silence. I was quietly thinking how much I was going to miss this place when he began to speak.

"You're traveling alone," he said with no question mark attached.

"Yes."

"Good for you. You're very close with your mother, aren't you? You're more friends than mother and child."

I was a bit taken aback by the randomness and the accuracy of his statement. "Yes."

We walked in silence for several minutes before he spoke again. "The world knocks you down and you come up smiling . . . you don't let it get you down. That's an admirable quality." And then he stopped and looked me right in the eyes. "Something happened to you a few years ago that would have been the end of most people . . . but not you. You know, it's all temporary and passes, and you smile because you know."

We walked a few more steps, then he stopped me again. "You're a beautiful person," he said, and then he gestured to his face. "And I don't mean this. Just remember that and keep smiling."

And with that, he deposited me at my destination and disappeared.

AFTERTHOUGHT

In 2008 (four years after the accident), I finished writing *Hot Cripple* as a one-woman show. My old acting coach let me come back to his class for free to develop all the characters I would be playing, and I was accepted to perform the show at the New York Fringe Festival, one of the largest theater festivals in the United States. I was finally going to tell my story to the world—and I was having doubts:

What if my story is boring?

What if I can't remember all my lines? Forty-two pages of script is rather ambitious for a girl who had a head injury.

Am I crazy to even attempt this?

Even Meryl Streep doesn't play twenty-five characters in a performance. What if I suck?

It was too late to turn back. My mom was flying in for the last performance; my brother, friends, and acquaintances had already bought their tickets; and then I received an email from my long out-of-contact friend Gayle. "Got your blast email about the show and am flying in to see it on Friday. Would love to catch up if you have the time. If not, no worries. I'm so proud of you."

After the Friday show Gayle came backstage with tears in her eyes and flowers in her hand. "I really felt like I wanted to vomit hearing what you've been through. I had no idea how bad it was. I stopped talking to you because you never asked about my pregnancy or how the baby was. I didn't know that you just couldn't remember."

I laughed as I gave her a hug. "I guess I forgot to tell you that I was forgetting a lot of things." Then I looked at her. "Wait, you had a baby? Can I see some pictures?"

Every performance was packed. A fire alarm went off during my last show. Thinking that someone had probably opened an emergency exit and that it would stop in a second, I continued my performance until the theater manager announced that there really was a fire and that we would have to evacuate the building. I went out on the sidewalk with my mom, my brother, Gayle, and the rest of the audience. Half an hour and three fire trucks later we were back in the theater. A man approached me. "Are you going to be okay to perform the rest of the show?" I gave him a wink and a smile. "I'll be fine. I've been through a lot worse." And with that I walked on stage and looked at the audience. "Well, now you know why they call me *Hot* Cripple," and I picked up the show right where I left off.

That night at the award ceremony for the Fringe, we were packed in like sardines. With two hundred and fifty shows in competition and about fifteen hundred actors, no surprise it was crowded. My mom went outside to get some air, and then they announced, "And the Outstanding Actor award goes to Hogan Gorman."

"That's you! They said your name!" Gayle shrieked. I fought my way to the stage and grabbed my award and went outside to find my mom.

"Mom. I won."

"Crap. I knew I should have stayed in there, but I was afraid I was going to faint. It's like when you won your first track meet and I was on the other side of the damn field. I never get to see my baby win."

"But you're the only reason I do win." And then I handed the award to my mom. "This is yours."

"Really? I can have it? Are you sure?"

"Positive. I wouldn't be here if it wasn't for you, and besides, I think Spike has more boastful wall space in your house than I do. This'll even it up a bit. What do you say we ladies go back to my place for a little chardonnay therapy?"

"Not only are you an award-winning actor, but you're brilliant. Let's get the hell out of here . . . Mama needs her medicine. By the way, when you win the Oscar, I want that, too."

My mother might be waiting a lifetime for that one . . . but hell, you never know.

In 2010, I put up the show again to full houses, and the publishing world came knocking, but something even more rewarding happened. After the show, I typically went out and greeted guests and well-wishers, and people who wanted to talk about the issues my show raises. That night I took my time packing up my stuff in the dressing room after the crowds had left, and as I exited the theater, a woman and her preteen daughter approached me. They both had huge smiles on their faces.

"Can I talk to you?" the woman asked.

"Of course you can."

"I normally don't go to the theater, but the woman I work for bought us tickets."

"I'm really happy you came."

"Watching you up there brought back everything that my family and I have been through with health care and welfare. People don't know unless they've been there, but you're taking them there, for all of us. Thank you," she said, giving me a hug.

That brief encounter and her words made it all worthwhile, for the chance to make one person feel less alone.

Since my accident and the aftermath, some things have changed for the worse and some for the better in this country. When the car hit me, we sued the driver, but the driver had a very low basic insurance policy, so we also sued the leasing company. Until recently, victims of automobile accidents in New York (and about eleven other states) had protection through vicarious liability, which allowed victims of car accidents to hold the owner of the car liable in cases that involved negligence, even if the owner wasn't the driver. In short, you could sue the leasing company or the rental company because they have control over who drives their cars. This law protected the victims; however, this has changed in recent years. Congress passed the Highway Bill, and hidden in this nine-hundred-page document was something called the Graves Amendment. The Graves Amendment does away with vicarious liability, and lets leasing and auto rental companies completely off the hook for any responsibility when someone driving one of their cars is negligent. The Graves Amendment was never debated on the floor of Congress, so those opposed to it were never allowed to argue for the rights of the victims.

So let me give you an example of how this amendment could affect you. Let's say you're out for a Sunday stroll, and you get hit by a car and are severely injured. This accident has left you in constant pain for the rest of your life, or even worse, let's say you lost a limb. The driver that hit you was driving a rental car or a leased car; he has no insurance and no personal assets . . . where does that leave you? Shit out of luck is where. It shouldn't be called the Graves Amendment, it should be called "You'll wish that car had put you in the grave." The National Highway Traffic Safety Administration reported that 4,092 pedestrians were killed and 59,000 were injured in 2009 (the most recent statistic I could find). The percentage of those injured left without the ability to obtain recompense for their injuries is probably more than I care to imagine.

As I sit here writing this, I am currently uninsured because I didn't make enough money with SAG (Screen Actors Guild) this year to be covered under their health plan, and no other insurance companies will cover my preexisting condition. I am, however, hopeful that someday soon this discrimination will be a thing of the past. On March 23, 2010 (six years and nineteen days after my accident), the Patient Protection and Affordable Care Act was signed into law. On the most elementary level, the law will guarantee that people can get more affordable health insurance, even if their employer does not insure them. This law prohibits insurers from denying coverage or charging more because of a person's health. This law requires individuals to have insurance, which spreads the cost of care among the healthy and the sick, which will ultimately bring down the cost of insurance (the more people insured, the lower the cost). It will also extend Medicaid to more people who can't afford to pay for insurance (with incomes at or below 133 percent of the federal poverty level), and close the prescription doughnut hole for people on Medicare.

Some Republicans in Congress and elsewhere have called this health care reform "Obamacare"; they tried to scare the masses with such sound bites as "Death Panels" and "pulling the plug on Grandma." It did, however, pass in 2010 with a Democratic majority in both the House and the Senate. So if everything remains intact, by the year 2014, adults with preexisting conditions will be able to have affordable health care, and discrimination by insurance companies will be a thing of the past, but how many people will die before 2014 remains to be seen. It is, however, a start and something that can be built on for years to come. As Ted Kennedy said, "Don't let perfect stand in the way of good."

After the November 2010 elections, Republicans gained control of the House, and the Senate remained under Democratic control. It is no surprise that the House GOP budget proposal for 2012 sought several different provisions intended to cut government costs, or that one of these proposals is to repeal the Affordable Care Act (ACA), including the Medicaid expansion that it authorizes. It also has separate proposals specifically for cutting federal funding for Medicaid, and others on Medicare. The proposed cuts to Medicare and Medicaid are $1.43 trillion combined.

The big Medicare cuts are only part of the Republican House budget proposal. This proposal also seeks to privatize Medicare by turning it into a voucher program. These vouchers would be the equivalent of eight thousand dollars and would be given to seniors so that they could take them and purchase private insurance on their own. However, the amount of these vouchers would not grow over time, meaning any increase in the cost of health care would be borne by the seniors themselves. This would without a doubt mean greater out-of-pocket costs. It would repeal the ACA and thus remove the provision that seeks to close the doughnut hole. This would not only raise costs for current beneficiaries by keeping the doughnut hole open, but it would raise the costs for future beneficiaries (who would get vouchers instead of Medicare) because they would be at the mercy of private insurance companies. The Center for Economic Policy Research recently put out a report that studied the effects that the House Budget Proposal would have on seniors. This report found that under the House budget proposal, the cost of a Medicare plan in 2022 would be 35 percent of the average sixty-five-year-old's income, and by 2050 it would be 68 percent.

Then there are the proposed cuts to Medicaid. According to the Kaiser Commission, as of 2011, Medicaid provides health coverage to about sixty million individuals: one in three children (60 percent of all low-income children), four in ten births, and 70 percent of nursing home residents. The House budget proposal aims to convert Medicaid to a block grant program, which will significantly cut federal funding for state Medicaid programs. These cuts would be phased in over a ten-year period: 5 percent in 2013 and increasing to 33 percent in 2021. Should the ACA be repealed, this would add another 13 percent in federal funding cuts, amounting to 44 percent in funding cuts over ten years. Presumably, the loss of federal funding for state programs, particularly during a time of increased state budget shortfalls, will result in many Americans losing health coverage. It is unrealistic to think that families at these extremely low income levels will be able to afford going from free coverage through Medicaid to potentially paying hundreds of dollars per year for private coverage on the exchange. As it stands, those eligible for Medicaid make up roughly 30 percent of the forty-seven million or so uninsured (presumably more if you take into consideration the Medicaid expansion allowed under the ACA).

The general public supports the public safety net and the retirement systems. These are the two main federal public health insurance programs in this country. Both Medicaid and Medicare are in the business of providing health care, not in the business of making profits. These two programs use the vast majority of their funding for providing health care to beneficiaries, and only a small amount goes to program administration. On the other hand, private insurance companies typically spend smaller amounts on providing actual health care and larger amounts on administration (including advertising, profits, and big CEO salaries).

In addition, the House GOP budget proposal would cut food stamps by $127 billion, which is almost 20 percent over the next ten years. From October 2007 (just before the financial crisis) to December 2010, the number of people on food stamps rose 62 percent to 44.1 million. These cuts would result in millions of low-income families being thrown off food stamps, or having their benefits drastically cut, increasing hunger and poverty during difficult economic times. Yes, this proposal sounds a lot like Marie Antoinette in a "let them eat cake" sort of way.

Although this budget plan was approved in the House, it has no real chance of passing in the Senate, so it is not likely to be adopted, but it's a sign of the possible future of our health care and welfare system should those who want to gut it be afforded the chance. By the time you are reading this book, we may be in the midst of yet another health care debate.

I recently read an article about a fifty-nine-year-old man in North Carolina who robbed a bank for one dollar in order to get arrested, so that he could go to prison to get treatment for an undiagnosed growth in his chest, two ruptured discs, and a problem with his foot. He said it was the only way he could get health care, after his medical ailments ended his seventeen-year career driving a Coca-Cola delivery truck. Yes, it is that bad out there. We can't let it get any worse.

On a good day I forget that a car hit me. There are still things that I can't do: go for the long runs I used to enjoy, carry anything heavy, play sports; and a career as a stunt man is definitely out of the question. And on a bad day, when my back is going out like Prada's last collection, I say to myself, "Self . . . stand up. You're not hurt. I'm a doctor. I know you're not hurt." And then I laugh until the pain goes away.

ACKNOWLEDGMENTS

This book was written entirely in long hand because I type about five words a minute. Thankfully, I print well, but I can't spell "shit" even if I'm standing in it. I would like to give a huge thanks to Dan Meyer for typing my book and deciphering the hieroglyphics that I call spelling. And when Dan told me he was over it and me, Lucy Poe stepped in for one chapter, so a big thanks to her. Dan eventually began to type again, but some major ass-kissing had to ensue first. To my mother, for spell-checking every chapter, even when she thought she was going to get fired from her job for printing it out on company paper. If there are any misspelled words it is her fault, and you should rat on her to her boss immediately. To my agent, Monika Verma, who came to my one-woman show and then stalked me until I finished my book proposal. To my editor, Jeanette Shaw, for putting up with my nervous break-downs and pulling me off my soapbox when I got carried away; she carries a mighty editing machete. To Arianne Slagle and Elisabeth Benjamin, for answering all my questions about the proposed cuts to Medicaid and Medicare, and explaining it so that a three-year-old could understand it. To Legal Eagle, for walking me through hell and then clarifying certain legal aspects for me, so that I could explain them to the reader. And lastly to the universe: The change you gave me wasn't really the change I had in mind, but I guess you were thinking outside the box . . . or should I say, windshield.